Workin' Hard for the Money:
The Social and Economic Lives of Women Drug Sellers

Workin' Hard for the Money:
The Social and Economic Lives of Women Drug Sellers

Ira Sommers, Deborah Baskin and Jeffrey Fagan

Nova Science Publishers, Inc.
Huntington, New York

Editorial Production:	Susan Boriotti
Office Manager:	Annette Hellinger
Graphics:	Frank Grucci
Information Editor:	Tatiana Shohov
Book Production:	Donna Dennis, Patrick Davin, Cathy DeGregory, and Lynette Van Helden
Circulation:	Latoya Clay and Anna Cruz

Library of Congress Cataloging-in-Publication Data

Sommers, Ira Brant.
    Workin' hard for the money : the social and economic lives of women drug sellers / Ira Sommers, Deborah Baskin, Jeffrey Fagan.
        p.   cm.
    Includes bibliographical references and index.
    ISBN 1-56072- 820-5
    1. Women narcotics dealers--New York (State)--New York--Social conditions. 2. Women narcotics dealers--New York (State)--New York—Economic conditions. 3. Narcotics and crime--New York (State)--New York. I. Baskin, Deborah R. II. Fagan, Jeffrey. III. Title.
HV5833.N45 S65   2000   00-033955
364.1'77'082097471--dc21   CIP

Copyright 2000 by Nova Science Publishers, Inc.
    227 Main Street, Suite 100
    Huntington, New York 11743
    Tele. 631-424-6682 Fax 631-424-4666
    e-mail: Novascience@earthlink.net
    e-mail: Novascil@aol.com
    Web Site: http://www.nexusworld.com/nova

All rights reserved. No part of this book may be reproduced, stored in a retrieval system or transmitted in any form or by any means: electronic, electrostatic, magnetic, tape, mechanical photocopying, recording or otherwise without permission from the publishers.

The authors and publisher have taken care in preparation of this book, but make no expressed or implied warranty of any kind and assume no responsibility for any errors or omissions. No liability is assumed for incidental or consequential damages in connection with or arising out of information contained in this book.

This publication is designed to provide accurate and authoritative information with regard to the subject matter covered herein. It is sold with the clear understanding that the publisher is not engaged in rendering legal or any other professional services. If legal or any other expert assistance is required, the services of a competent person should be sought. FROM A DECLARATION OF PARTICIPANTS JOINTLY ADOPTED BY A COMMITTEE OF THE AMERICAN BAR ASSOCIATION AND A COMMITTEE OF PUBLISHERS.

Printed in the United States of America

Contents

Chapter 1:	Introduction	1
Chapter 2:	Structure, Culture and Opportunity: Explaining the Feminization of Drug Markets	15
Chapter 3:	Neighborhood, Family and School	27
Chapter 4:	Initiation Into and the Context of Drug Dealing	49
Chapter 5:	Legal and Illegal Work: Work, Crime and Drug Dealing	73
Chapter 6:	Living the Life	87
Chapter 7:	Quitting the Life	109
Chapter 8:	Conclusions	127
Appendix 1:	The Sample	145
Appendix 2:	The Relationship Between Drug Dealing and other Money Making Activities	151
References		163
Index		179

Chapter 1

INTRODUCTION

THE CHANGING FACE OF DRUG MARKETS

I just got out of prison and I asked my sister how much it would cost to start a business. She said $500. I got a grand from my husband. I bought 2 ounces of cooked up crack. Opened this place at one of my sister's friend's house. She was strung out on crack. I already mastered a plan for it. I just paid the girl crack. I didn't have to pay her cash for the apartment. I started making good money. I wasn't using crack at the time. I did begin to use it about a year later. Soon after, me and my sister was smoking $1500 worth of crack a day. It wasn't even hurting the profits.

I had a little crew. About eight of us: seven women. I always had a dream to have an all women crew. Whether people realize it or not, women sell drugs more easily than men. More people approach you because you are a woman. Usually women don't like to be known selling drugs so sometimes they have a male front. There are a lot of woman drug dealers. They have males to front off for them, to keep attention off of them. You have to have some type of protection over yourself. a man who they believe is the boss.

(Denise)

In the above account, Denise suggests that women have created substantial roles within drug markets; roles that are not subordinate to their male counterparts. This perception of women as principals in drug markets contradicts a fair amount of research and conventional wisdom. Research in this area, for instance, argues that women's drug activities are heavily linked to male partners. Women are portrayed in this literature as occupying assistant roles, helping male drug dealers by touting products, steering customers to them, or by holding drugs or related illegal paraphernalia (Adler, 1985; Lyman and Potter, 1991; Mieczkowski, 1986).

Furthermore, the public's beliefs about drug dealers have been consistent with these research findings. For most people, their image of a drug dealer is a BMW-driving, Timberland-attired, gun-toting, *male*. They see women's involvement in drug markets as peripheral. Instead, the public is more likely to conceive of women as drug abusers, prostitutes, check forgers, and welfare frauds, existing on the perimeters of drug markets, drawn into the setting by virtue of their associations with drug dealing pimps, brothers, boyfriends, or husbands.

However, during the late 1980s, we took notice of a phenomenon that had been emerging in New York City since the mid-80s: the growth of direct female involvement in drug selling. Arrest, detention, and sentencing data, as well as newspaper and magazine stories, were slowly revealing a new picture of urban drug markets. This picture began to include women sellers, women crew bosses, and queen pins. Clearly, though, women were not taking over the markets. But, they were entering distribution settings in greater numbers and in more ways than existed previously. As a result, the dealing subcultures formed during the mid to late 1980s were more multifaceted and diverse than had been depicted in prevailing research and public discourse.

Despite these changes, much of the literature on criminal careers such as drug dealing, continued, through the 80s and 90s, to focus on men. Several factors account for the lack of attention that was being paid to the dealing careers of women. Perhaps most important among them was a quantitative argument. The fact that men outnumbered women in participation was used to justify the depiction of women's careers either as anomalies or as forms of "secondary deviance" within domestic partnerships (Campbell 1993; Pettiway 1987). Thus, women's involvement in dealing, as in most street crimes, was reported as being an adjunct to, or in support of, male careers. When a "few" female cases were examined, explanations for them focused on dealing as an example of gender role deviance rather than as a violation of conventional or legal norms, as was the case for males. In this way female involvement was trivialized and explained away as insignificant, or inconsequential, especially as compared to women's addiction problems.

Even when it came to addiction, though, the literature on women's drug abuse careers emerged from research conducted with males, especially of men who were involved in heroin (e.g., Becker 1963; Preble and Casey 1969;

Waldorf 1973; Agar 1973). Despite the fact that many of these studies reported that male addicts committed violent crimes, sold drugs, and were clearly lawbreakers, the literature on women continued to portray them as "deviant" and not criminal. Women drug addicts had embarked on careers of deviance from gender roles. They were a public health threat because of their drug use during pregnancy, and a mental health threat due to their psychopathology (Colten and Marsh 1984). They were bad mothers, bad wives, bad daughters or madwomen, but never criminal. They may have been minor hustlers or prostitutes (Miller 1986; Waterston 1993) but nothing more significant. They hustled and hooked to support their own addictions and sometimes the habits of their current, mostly male, partners (Hunt 1990; Inciardi, Lockwood and Potteiger 1993). But again, their actions were inconsequential relative to their male counterparts. Studies on women and drug abuse further mirrored the dealing literature by repeating the timeworn formula of women's involvement as being initiated by males through domestic or friendship networks (Rosenbaum 1981).

These notions about women's careers in drugs were situated in times and places characterized by specific structural factors and social contexts. Nonetheless, macro-level changes in community and drug market environments during the 1980s and early 90s altered women's using and selling careers. As cocaine replaced heroin as the primary drug in street markets, and as the age-gender composition of inner cities shifted, women became more extensively involved in drug selling than in previous drug "eras" (Baskin, Sommers and Fagan 1993).

By the mid-to late 1980s, women's roles and experiences in drug selling changed. They were moving away from adjunct selling-hustling roles to more systematic and sometimes "high stakes" forms of participation. Some women earned substantial incomes from drug selling. As a result, they were able to buy some protection from exploitation in sex markets (Fagan 1994). Some women were even able to avoid prostitution, altogether, while others were able to leave it (Sommers, Baskin, and Fagan, 1996)--in many ways because of the new opportunities afforded them in the 1980s drug markets.

By and large, three factors that emerged during the 1980s changed the dynamics and contexts of drug use and selling for women. First, the increased availability of inexpensive cocaine products, especially cheap smokable cocaine, made possible serious drug use without the risks of injection or physiological addiction (Bourgois 1989; Hamid 1990; Waldorf, Reinarman and Murphy 1991). Smoking cocaine also carried with it the risk of high rate drug use and dependency (Siegel 1987; Reinarman et al. 1989; Williams 1992). The expansion of cocaine markets and the lower price of cocaine created new forms of drug selling for both men and women (Johnson, Hamid and Morales 1990; Fagan 1992; Baskin, Sommers and Fagan 1993). Easier access to cocaine accelerated the developmental progression from "gateway" use of alcohol and marijuana to serious drug use among both men and women, and may have contributed to more prevalent and frequent cocaine use in inner cities (Golub and Johnson 1993).

Second, significant structural shifts in the social and economic compositions of inner cities changed the social organization of drug use and selling (Johnson et al. 1990; Fagan 1992; Fagan and Chin 1991. The loss of millions of manufacturing jobs in large cities since the 1960s (Kasarda 1988) led to dramatic shifts in the gender/age composition of inner city neighborhoods. The proportion of adult males to females declined sharply from 1960 to 1980, and the proportion of female-headed households substantially increased (Wilson 1987; Wacquant and Wilson 1989).[1] Many of these households had incomes below the poverty line (Jencks and Peterson 1991), and participation in the growing informal economy in inner cities became part of the diverse network of income sources for poor women (Sassen-Koob 1989). The influences of "female old heads" on young women also weakened as neighborhoods grew poorer and younger (Anderson 1990). With the expansion of the drug economy and its opportunities for "crazy money" (Williams 1989) street-smart girls (and boys) rejected the old heads' lessons about life and the work ethic. Thus, changes in population composition and labor market access may have weakened the informal controls that regulated drug networks and the people who participate in them.

Third, the demand for cheap cocaine products in the 1980s exceeded the capacity of existing drug distribution systems. This created new opportunities for both men and women to buy and sell cocaine and other drugs (Johnson et al. 1990; Goldstein et al. 1991). The growing cocaine economy improved access to supplies, expanded entry-level roles in drug distribution, made possible entry into drug selling with a small capital investment, and generated

---

[1] These jobs were important points of entry into labor market participation for working class men and women. Blue collar employment provided the basis, among minorities in poor neighborhoods, for the expectation of social mobility and steady if not spectacular wages over the work career (Farley, 1987; Farley and Allen 1987).

"controlled" selling territories with guaranteed incomes (Hamid 1990; Williams 1989; Johnson et al. 1990). Thus, the cocaine economy of the 1980s opened the doors for scores of women to enter into criminal enterprises and street networks in new ways and in greater numbers.

This book examines women's participation in the cocaine/crack economy of New York City. All the women you will read about are or were long-term drug dealers, not those who casually dealt drugs. In order to be included in our study, a person had to have sold drugs for at least two years. Many of our respondents were involved in drug distribution for considerably longer periods. Thus, the voices heard here are of those who had substantial drug selling careers.

In this book, we seek to describe the lives of women drug dealers- not so much from our point of view as from their own. In the research undertaken, we sought to listen to the women and understand the cultural perspectives through which they created their lives. Thus, we represent the women as responsive subjects and present their world as close as possible to how they saw it. Throughout the book, the women describe their experiences through their own vernacular. Telling their stories in this way, we create a text full of complexity and richness of meaning in which the street drug and criminal subculture is understood through the words of those who usually are spoken for, studied and objectified.

Unlike other qualitative works in this area, we provide more than cultural analysis. We integrate structural and individual levels of explanation by examining the career patterns of female drug dealers and the relationships of these women to other members of their communities. Through the use of census data, analyses of political and economic changes and ethnographic observations of activities specific to these communities, we provide a perspective on the relation of individual decisions to structural constraints. It is the interweaving of the structural and individual levels of analysis that has been missing from most studies of crime and drugs. We view the community as a locus of interaction, intermediate between the individual and the larger society, where many constraints and opportunities of the total society are narrowed to a subset within which local individuals choose. The local community is also the cultural milieu within which the value of these options is defined.

OVERVIEW OF THE BOOK

This book has three interrelated directions. First, we examine how processes of urban structural and economic decay have combined to create new and invigorate old criminogenic factors. We identify factors that cut across gender categories (e.g. peers general drug abuse, victimization, criminal opportunities) and others that apply primarily to women (e.g. decline in family and neighborhood supervision, earlier termination of education, and crack addiction). These factors have resulted in dramatic changes in women's participation in street crime. Second, we explore how personal decisions related to such participation are mediated by women's experiences and understanding of their present environment. And, third, we are interested in developing a framework for understanding how the *interaction* between personal history, social processes, and a changing inner city structures women's participation in drug selling. More specifically, early socialization experiences (child abuse and neglect, family, peer and community networks) substance abuse and criminal careers, and the movement in and out of conventional activities (education, legitimate employment) are linked to broader social, economic and situational processes.

In Chapter Two we offer a social structural explanation for the expansion of female involvement in drug dealing. This explanation roots the drug problem squarely within the everyday life experiences of women growing up in underclass communities. For, regardless of race, age or gender, people from underclass communities are involved disproportionately in street drug selling.

But how does residence in areas characterized by high concentrations of poverty influence *women's* decisions to participate in drug dealing? In Chapter Three, we present the women's descriptions of how living in communities distinguished by their intensified economic and social dislocation, growing drug markets, demographic changes and situational factors related to family, school and peer relations contributed to their participation in drug markets.

In this chapter, we also examine how changes in the strength and composition of family networks and relations, as well as the decline in prosocial role models and community institutions combine to "liberate" these women from the traditional gender-based constraints on involvement in drug markets.

In many ways, this chapter offers the strongest challenge to the traditional perspective on female offending. Although we do not discount the role that victimization and drug abuse play in the **careers** of **some** women engaged in drug selling, the women we interviewed offer different perspectives on how direct a role, if any, these factors played in terms of their own **initiation** into drug dealing. These perspectives were frequently at variance with the more traditional explanations.

Chapter Four examines the processes of entry and initiation into drug selling. An important controversy in the literature on women and drugs was the routes they took to drug selling. Some have characterized it as a process of drift, while others have rejected drift in favor of explanations based on economic determinism or truncated choices dictated by the demands of drug use or family obligations. This chapter carefully fashions the processes of entry into drug selling based on understanding the complex pulls and pushes on women's lives at the several stages preceding their involvement in selling. The casual processes of holding paraphernalia or drugs typify one process of entry, based on immersion in street networks of drug users or involvement in domestic arrangements with male drug users or sellers. The entrepreneurial processes of multiplying a small investment into a lucrative direct sales enterprise is another scenario. A third scenario involves multiple criminal enterprises, where drug selling is situated in a diverse set of illegal means of income production.

In this chapter, we also analyze the social context of drug selling. We examine the organizational roles that typified the women's involvement in drug markets and we examine the use of violence in the context of drug dealing, the pharmacological effects of certain drugs on participation in street crime, and the extent to which the women were victimized by virtue of being sellers and/or users.

Many of the women we interviewed reported that their initiation into drugs was due to many of the same sets of factors that accounted for the initiation of their male counterparts--e.g. peers, search for excitement and adventure, opportunity structures and neighborhood effects. Weak attachments to prosocial institutions, lack of positive parental supervision, associations with deviant peers and other social and economic processes prevalent in severely distressed communities lay the groundwork for increased female involvement in drug distribution. The women we spoke with described, in great detail the role that these neighborhood effects played in their initiation.

At least initially, the majority of the women we interviewed attempted to become involved in the legal job market. At the same time, however, making money remained tied to their concern with living large. Concerns over these two spheres of activity are explored in Chapters Five. These concerns helped to define their cultural lives--how the women spent time, forms of self-expressions and identity, public and private moments and the use of drugs and drinking. Ultimately, the deviant street network takes increasingly prominence in their quest for self-identity and expression.

The focus of Chapter Six is on the effects of involvement in drug markets on women's social and economic options. We assume that decisions to become involved in drug markets are shaped initially by choices within the neighborhood contexts, and are mediated later by the exigencies and demands of the drug markets themselves. Women's immersion in street networks where drugs are used and traded is examined within the perspective of *role engulfment* -- a reciprocal social process where behaviors and social options are narrowed continually by the logic of the social context that demands full time participation for "success."

Despite the fact that these women's lives were filled with crime, drugs and violence, there were some who eventually exited from their criminal and drug careers. In Chapter seven, we describe the social processes and turning points that triggered these women's exits from street deviance. We conclude the chapter with the presentation of a three-stage model for understanding desistance from drug dealing.

In the conclusion, we deconstruct the concept of female offender in order to better appreciate the complexity of women's involvement in drug careers. Further, we emphasize the importance of the developmental perspective on the timing and sequence of initiation into drug selling, use, and crime. Finally, we assess contemporary policies regarding drugs, especially in terms of gender.

A NOTE ON RESEARCH METHODS

Our research was based primarily on in-depth, life-history interviews with 156 women who sold drugs in two New York City neighborhoods: Washington Heights, in northern Manhattan, and Bushwick, in central Brooklyn. Each neighborhood had active heroin markets in the 1970s and also were the flash points for the growth of cocaine and crack markets a decade later (Sviridoff, Sadd, Curtis, and Grinc 1992).

The women were recruited from various social settings where female sellers were likely to be located, including: (1) those currently not in jail or treatment, and who were active in drug selling in these two neighborhoods; (2) those in jail for drug sale convictions; and (3) those in state prison for drug sale convictions.

Street Samples

Street samples were recruited through chain referral or "snowball" sampling procedures (Biernacki and Waldorf 1981; Watters and Biernacki 1989), techniques appropriate for "hidden" populations whose population parameters are not well known. Women drug sellers in these markets were not well represented in official records, and typified the problems of transience that complicate research with drug users (Dunlap et al., 1990; Lewis, Johnson, Golub and Dunlap, 1992). Women currently involved in drug trade were recruited through arrangements with fieldworkers active in ethnographic research in both Washington Heights and Bushwick. These ongoing studies were designed to collect data on drug sales/distribution, drug use and non-drug criminality. For example, one study was concerned with vectors of HIV transmission through intravenous drug users and crack users. Another was an outreach and drug prevention effort using street contacts to deliver services to people involved in drug use. Although these projects did not focus specifically on female dealers, they had established a strong field presence that provided fairly easy access to non-arrested neighborhood female drug dealers. Forty percent (N=63) of the interviews were conducted with active drug dealers; the rest were conducted in institutional settings.

Incarcerated Samples

Active caseload lists of women incarcerated for drug sale convictions at New York State and City correctional facilities were used to select our incarcerated samples. Correctional records were reviewed in order to develop a pool of women from the two respective neighborhoods. Screening interviews with the potential respondents also were used to ensure that the research participants resided in the two study neighborhoods. Forty percent (N=62) of the interviews were conducted with women incarcerated in state prison and 20% (N=31) with women in jail.

Sample Description

The typical respondent in our study was a minority woman (African-American or Latina), in her early 30s, who dropped out of high school, possessed limited legal work experience, and had two children. The youngest respondent was 16 years old and the oldest 48; the median age was 30 years. Three in four women were high school dropouts, typically leaving school by eleventh grade. Although most of the women had worked in a legitimate job (83%), the median number of total months employed was only 24, the average was 42.97 months. More than four in five respondents (88%) worked in unskilled and semiskilled working-class occupations (e.g., clerical and factory jobs).

The women were engaged in a wide range of criminal and deviant activities. Nearly all said they were experienced drug users. Seventy percent were regular crack users, 47% used cocaine regularly and 41% were at some point in time addicted to heroin. Of the 156 women we interviewed, 38% reported involvement in robbery, 17% reported involvement in burglary, 33% had committed assault, and 44% were at sometime involved in prostitution.

The women in this study sold multiple drugs. Many diversified or changed their products over time. Most (81%) of the women had sold crack. About half (52% and 45%) had sold heroin and cocaine, respectively. The average age of initiation into dealing was before 25 years of age. Most had been selling for at least five years.

Interview Procedures

For respondents residing in the community, interviews were conducted in a neutral location such as a library, coffee shop or private office. In order to convey the neutrality and anonymity of the study, we avoided offices of either criminal justice agencies or clinical settings. Respondents were given a stipend of $30 for the interview. For women who were incarcerated, all attempts were made to conduct interviews in as private a setting as possible within the correctional facility. These women did not receive a stipend due to institutional rules.

The two hour interviews were open-ended, in-depth and audio taped. These procedures created an atmosphere where respondents could speak freely and in their own words. It also facilitated detailed discussion of issues that were raised by the women during the interview but were not recognized beforehand by the researcher. We were able to produce information about specific events, as well as provide an opportunity for respondents to reflect on those events. Finally, tape recording allowed interviewers to adopt a more conversational style and devote his/her complete attention to the respondent, avoiding the intrusion of writing down lengthy responses.

Time reference points were used to assist in the recall of information. The method of sequencing the interview into intervals that are meaningful to the respondent has yielded valid and rich retrospective, longitudinal data covering long periods of time (Anglin and Hser, 1987). The procedure requires that the interviewer work closely with the respondent to structure the period of interest, using corroborative information and memory aids (e.g. life events and associated dates from official records). In this way, criminal behavior patterns and displacement, shifts in the frequency or severity of criminal involvement (lulls, episodes, relapses after lengthy desistance periods) and contributing situational factors (peer group roles, legal or social sanctions, and life events such as the birth of a child or loss of a job) can be temporally anchored over a multiyear period to establish the natural history of criminal behavior and the factors that have affected its course.

The interview began by reviewing with the women issues of sponsorship, purpose of the research, the selection procedure, anonymity of respondent's interviews, and the purpose of taping. The interviewer answered questions pertaining to the selection process, the nature of the study, and so on. The interviewer emphasized the confidentiality of the interview and pointed out that a code number, rather than the respondent's name, is used to identify the interview. Following this introduction, the respondent was asked to participate by signing a consent form that summarized the assurances contained in the opening statement.

A life history approach was used to describe initiation into dealing and involvement with drugs, the social processes of selling and drug use, income sources from both legitimate and illegal activities, and non-drug criminality. Detailed questions were asked about specific drugs and crimes, frequencies of involvement, expenditures/income, and transitions from initiation to regular involvement to cessation.

For initiation, respondents were asked to describe how, where, with whom, and why they initially sold drugs, their expectations and reactions to dealing, how much money they made, and their involvement in other criminal activities. Social history data also were obtained, including quality of interpersonal relations, nature of social networks, level of acculturation of ethnic minority members, drug use and dealing history of the social group.

The social organization of drug selling included several types of information. Respondents were asked whether they sold drugs as part of an organization, to describe their organization, to report their specific roles in drug selling and roles that were evident in the selling organization, and social processes that existed within their group.

The economic lives of respondents were described through questions on income and expenditures. Monthly dollar amounts were reported for the year dealing was initiated and for three subsequent years. Dollar estimates were recorded for both legitimate and illegal sources of income, and for expenditures both for living costs and drugs.

The interviews yielded information about patterns of drug use and treatment, including lifetime use, age at first use, age at first regular use, route of administration, and frequency and severity of current use for major classes of drugs, number of drugs used concurrently, and alcohol use, number and types of treatments, ages at which treatment was received, frequency and duration of treatment, motivation to enter previous and current treatment, factors that led to entering treatment, attrition from treatment, and factors that led to attrition.

Obtaining an independent means to test the validity of at least some portion of the self-report data was particularly desirable for this study because the information collected could easily have been subject to exaggeration or lack of recall. In the present research, estimates of individual offending patterns were confirmed independently through official arrest and conviction records. Official records data were used to help reduce response errors. Interviewers mentioned events found in the official record in order to trigger the recall of events and time periods as well as to curtail respondent misrepresentation of criminal activities.

Our interest in examining the pushes and pulls of the various social worlds encountered and experienced by these women was facilitated by the life history technique. Through these interviews, the women were able to represent to us a level of activity, creativity and human agency that might otherwise not have been attainable. It permitted us to understand how their experiences, relationships and other processes structurally and experientially established how the "choices" they faced emerged and how they were then defined. In this way, we were better able to understand how embedded their criminal careers were within larger social worlds that, by and large, reinforced their involvement.

The value of life history interviews in this process lies in the wealth of data that is collected as well as its usefulness in facilitating the development of "thick descriptions (Geertz, 1973)." With the assistance of highly trained interviewers, 156 women developed autobiographical accounts of their life experiences such that, now, we are better able to appreciate the *wide* range of everyday processes that contributed to the establishment and maintenance of their drug dealing careers.

Chapter 2

STRUCTURE, CULTURE AND OPPORTUNITY: EXPLAINING THE FEMINIZATION OF DRUG MARKETS

What led to the increased participation of women in New York City's drug markets? In answering this question, this chapter outlines a set of processes that pulled inner city women into drug dealing. Within a community context characterized by growing and changing drug markets, economic and social dislocation, and a marked disappearance of males, situational factors related to family, school and peer relations combined to create social and economic opportunity structures open to women's increasing participation in drug markets.

DRUG MARKETS: GROWTH AND CHANGE

The Heroin Era

Most explanations of women's involvement in drug markets are situated in the particular time and place of the heroin era, the 20 year period beginning in the early 1960s.[2] Rosenbaum's (1981) important study showed how

---

[2] See, for example: Clayton and Voss 1981; Hunt and Chambers 1976; Inciardi 1979.

involvement with heroin typically narrowed the options for income production and social interactions among women. Other studies of this time period continued the age old tradition of depicting deviant women, in this case, heroin users, as emotionally unstable and sexually promiscuous (Colten and Marsh 1984; Stephens 1991; Erickson and Murray 1991). In either portrayal, women's involvement in drug markets cut off their participation in conventional economic activities and in traditional social circles. Thus, these women existed outside of the pale of acceptable gendered behavior. However, even in their "deviance", the portrayals remained gender bound.

Nevertheless, drug selling in heroin markets was, indeed, a highly gendered activity (Preble and Casey 1969; Johnson et al. 1985; Adler 1985; Williams 1989, 1992). Women were rarely active for long periods in street drug selling, and domestic arrangements often mediated women's participation in both drug use and selling (Rosenbaum 1981; Valentine 1978; Miller 1986; Hunt 1990). For example, prior to the growth of street-level cocaine markets, women sellers usually were limited to roles as "holders" or peripheral members of male-dominated dealing groups (Goldstein 1979). Research on women and heroin suggest that being cut off from boyfriends/husbands who supplied the women's drug habits, forced women into drug dealing only until consistent access to drugs vis-a-vis a lover was restored (Adler 1985; Inciardi et al. 1993; Miller 1986; Rosenbaum 1981).

However, regular heroin use eventually reduced the stream of lovers needed to take care of them and their habits. Thus, over time, their involvement in social support networks became severely truncated. And, the income generating limitations within local drug markets for women meant that they could not rely solely on dealing to provide enough money to feed their habits. As a result, daily life for women heroin users eventually came down to the pursuit of money for drugs by any means necessary.

Gender played an important role in how these women negotiated the "street life" that accompanied regular heroin use. Although prostitution and other criminal activity often preceded involvement in heroin (and other street drugs), the heavy expenses of heroin use required a diverse array of income sources. Since heavy involvement as a user reduced the options for women to engage in legal work (Hunt 1990; Rosenbaum 1981), these incomes came mainly through illegal activity (Anglin and Hser 1987; Valentine 1978; Miller 1986). As heavy drug use increased, dependence on illegal incomes increased. Therefore, women often doubled up in drug distribution and prostitution both to "make a living" as well as to skim or buy drugs with their "profits" (Rosenbaum 1981; Miller 1986; Waterston 1993). Further, as involvement with heroin continued to increase, the gendered world of drug distribution made it difficult for women to make sufficient money to supply their drug needs (Adler 1985; Hser, Anglin & McGlothlin 1987). Access to supplies and viable roles in selling were difficult for women (Johnson et al. 1985). Although dealing provided access to small supplies of drugs, it provided little money for other needs. It was a less attractive economic choice than hustling, fraud, theft, or prostitution.

As part of their diverse income producing and drug procurement strategies, women often entered into crime partnerships with males. In these settings, women often were consigned to roles as lookouts while men did the heavy and sometimes violent work associated with criminal enterprise (Pettiway 1987). Women also played a passive role simply as holders and/or users of stolen property or drugs. Or, they were asked to provide support services for criminally active male members of domestic and boyfriend networks (Rosenbaum 1981). They also contributed their incomes from such crimes as fraudulent check cashing, prostitution, shoplifting, and other gendered types of criminal involvement, to their partner of the moment, And, they provided sex, food, and housekeeping for them, as well. (Adler 1985; Blom & van den Berg 1989; Miller 1986; Johnson et al. 1985; Steffensmeier 1983). But these relationships were exploitative. Women's incomes often supported either crime partnerships with men or men's drug use. They were rarely used to meet the women's own needs or to improve their own situations. Thus, the gender disparities in this informal economy mirrored the disadvantages of women in the formal economy.

During the heroin era, prostitution provided an income source that was perceived by women as perhaps preferable to other forms of "gendered" and very circumscribed illicit work. Hunt (1990) suggested that women turned from drug dealing and its limitations to prostitution because the latter was easier and more profitable. Despite the considerable risks of victimization from customers and pimps, women saw prostitution as less dangerous than drug dealing(Goldstein 1979; Cohen 1980; Maher and Curtis 1993; Williams 1992). But involvement in prostitution produced its own iatrogenic effects. It further narrowed the women's already disintegrating social networks. By abandoning crime partnerships and their social networks for higher incomes from prostitution, women faced a precipitous decline in their network of social contacts and support systems. Prostitution also led to the breakup of domestic relationships with husbands, boyfriends or lovers. This, in turn, further narrowed their social networks. The resulting marginalization also carried an increased risk of legal and social sanctions, including the loss of children, and health risks including higher rates of drug use, sexually transmitted diseases, and HIV infection (Longshore et al. 1993; French 1993). Thus, women's involvement with heroin often led to increasingly narrower options for income and for social interactions.

Over time, women heroin users moved into serious addiction careers through their participation in street hustles, deviant social networks, and crime partnerships with males. While hustling and other "gender-consistent" crimes supported drug use for both the woman and her partner, drug use eventually replaced the domestic/boyfriend arrangement for many women. Deepening involvement with drugs shaped economic decisions, too, making prostitution a more profitable alternative. Even women who avoided prostitution and earned incomes from selling drugs or other hustles suffered the presumption of prostitution and the social marginalization associated with it (Rosenbaum 1981). To the extent that social networks mediated involvements with heroin (Biernacki 1986), the closing off of income sources and social contacts made it difficult for women to extricate themselves from these narrowing options.

DRUG ERAS AND CHANGING STREET NETWORKS

By 1980, heroin use stabilized and even declined in inner cities. Heroin users became a small and aging group (see, for example: Boyle and Brunswick 1980; Goldstein et al. 1984; Johnson et al. 1990). There were only enough heroin initiates each year to replace those who died, or who were incarcerated, or who discontinued its use (Kleiman 1992). On the other hand, beginning in 1975, cocaine use rose (see, for example, Kozel and Adams 1985),[3] with the highest rates of cocaine powder use reported in the late 1970s

---

[3] Kleiman (1992), interpreting NIDA Household Survey data from 1982-90, claims that over 20 million Americans have used cocaine (in powder, freebase, or its crack forms) at least once, "several million use it at least occasionally, and between two and three million do so weekly or more..." (288). It would be a mistake to assume that among either males or females, cocaine use replaced heroin. Although many heroin users also used cocaine, often "speedballing" them together via injection, newer and younger cocaine initiates beginning in the late 1970s began cocaine use following progressions through alcohol and marijuana but

and early 1980s (Kleiman 1992). Crack emerged in New York City in 1985, and in other urban areas shortly afterward (Belenko, Fagan and Chin 1991).[4],[5] In New York City, street drug markets expanded from the small number of heroin locations to a diversified network of cocaine distribution points that at times resembled festive bazaars (Zimmer 1987).

As cocaine use supplanted heroin as the most widely used "serious" drug (Johnson et al. 1990; Kleiman 1992), the development of a cocaine economy among street drugs changed the contexts and dynamics of women's drug involvement. The unfolding of the cocaine HCL and crack eras unfolded brought changes in two dimensions that had shaped women's drug involvement in the past: the social contexts of drug use, and the drug itself.

---

not heroin (Kandel, Yamaguchi and Chen 1992; Fagan and Chin 1991). Cocaine in this period was used primarily through snorting cocaine powder (cocaine hydrochloride, or cocaine HCL) (Siegel 1987). After peaking in 1979 nationally, the prevalence of cocaine use quickly throughout the next decade (ONDCP 1989). But the declines through 1985 were far slower among two populations: "high rate" cocaine users, and poor and minority groups in inner cities (Johnson et al. 1990b). Crack emerged in New York's poorest neighborhoods in 1985, and in similar areas in other cities within a few years.

[4] At first, crack was sold in street drug markets in cities in or near cocaine importation points. See Inciardi et al. (1993) regarding Miami, and Klein, Maxson and Cunningham (1991) regarding Los Angeles. How quickly it spread to other cities is a matter of debate. For example, Ouellet et al. (1993) found few persons with street reputations for smoking crack prior to 1990, but they came into contact with crack users as their ethnographic work progressed.

[5] Most cocaine users had been aware of the intensified high experienced from smoking freebase cocaine (Siegel 1982; Waldorf et al. 1991). However, quantities of cocaine sufficient for "basing" had been beyond the economic means of most drug users. Crack became widely available in small quantities at low unit costs ($10 for three small rocks). Compared to the manufacture of freebase cocaine, the crack production process was cheaper, simpler, safer, and more efficient. Distribution points proliferated, including both street markets and indoor locations in the city's poorest neighborhoods (Fagan and Chin 1990; Johnson et al. 1990b). Crack houses sprang up as modern day opium dens (Hamid 1993; Bourgois 1989; Williams 1992), providing a controlled environment for crack use where supplies were limited only by the user's cash or ability to barter. Similar to its more expensive freebase form, crack cocaine posed considerable risk for compulsive use (Gawin & Kleber 1988; Siegel 1987; Spitz & Rosecan 1987). The intense crack high lasted a relatively short time (less than 20 minutes) and was followed by a sharp depression that led to a strong desire to get high again (Reinarman et al. 1989). Many users reported constantly "chasing" the initial euphoric high by continuing to smoke crack.

COCAINE, CRACK, AND DRUG MARKETS

The transition of street drug markets from heroin to cocaine and crack changed the social organization of drug use and selling (Johnson et al. 1990). Street-level drug selling in New York, for example, was a family-centered heroin and marijuana business until the 1980s, when new organizations developed to control distribution of cocaine (Johnson et al. 1990). Coupled with the structural and contextual changes in street drug networks, changes in drugs and drug markets made possible new avenues and contexts for women to participate in drug use and selling.

First, the psychoactive and physiological effects of cocaine were quite different from heroin. Cocaine is a short-acting central nervous system stimulant.[6] Cocaine effects are relatively short-lived, and the declining stimulation of pleasure centers leads to anxiety, edginess, and depression (Waldorf, et al. 1991). Users can ward off the effects of this "crash" by using more cocaine. Thus, cocaine sessions often entail binges of many hours of repeated use where sleep is obviated. The effects of smoking crack or cocaine freebase are more intense but similar. Reports from users suggest that smoking a rock of crack produced a brief (about 20 minutes) but intense high, followed by a "crash" and the rapid onset of depression with a compelling drive to get high again (Spitz and Rosecan 1987; Siegel 1987; Reinarman et al. 1989; Fagan and Chin 1991).

While heroin use involved a small number of consistent daily doses, cocaine and crack use were characterized by multiple purchases in relatively short periods of time. The psychoactive effects of heroin and its methods of administration limited the volume of sales and the number of users. But cocaine was different in every way: a stimulant rather than a depressant, ingested in a variety of ways (nasally, smoked, or injected), and with a shorter half-life for the high. Moreover, cocaine HCL was portrayed for many years as a "safe" drug that was not addictive, did not interfere with other social activities, and whose use could be easily self-controlled (Siegel 1987; Waldorf et al. 1991). The ability to use intense drugs without needles and therefore reduce the risk of HIV transmission, was an added appeal for some users

---

[6] Cocaine blocks the reabsorption of dopamine, a neurotransmitter chemical, into the neurons that release it. It thereby temporarily accelerates perception and thoughts. Cocaine is powerfully reinforcing, and both animal and human subjects who find that a given behavior will lead to a dose of cocaine will increase the frequency of that behavior (Gawin 1991).

(Fagan and Chin 1991). Accordingly, attractions of the drug itself made possible the entry of women in what they may have seen as a safer form of intense drug use.

Second, cocaine products became widely available as drug selling points. Organizations grew to meet the expanded demand (Zimmer 1987; Williams 1989). The cocaine HCL and crack markets were nurtured by customers making repeat purchases for lengthy sessions often lasting days. Demand for cocaine products was fueled by its short lasting effects, its relatively low unit cost ($10-20 for a vial with three rocks, or $10 for a small packet of powder), and its ease of use (no needles, only a pipe for smoking or tools for snorting). Thus, the interaction of the changing social circumstances of women in inner cities, the weakening of the dominance of males in street networks, and the expanded opportunities for cocaine use, made possible the initiation of women into serious drug use in ways far different from earlier drug eras.

Third, drug selling became an attractive income option for women with low educational levels and job skills, especially in the vastly shrinking labor market. They had several employment options within drug markets: support roles (lookout, tout), manufacturing (cut, package, weigh), or direct street sales (Johnson et al. 1990; Goldstein et al. 1991). In contrast, the heroin markets from the 1970s were far smaller than the cocaine HCL and crack markets, both in total volume of sales and the average purchase amount and quantity (Johnson et al. 1990).

Cocaine HCL and crack sales became institutionalized in New York City. In storefronts, from behind the counters in bodegas, on street corners, in crack or "freak" houses, and through several types of "fronts," drug selling was a common and visible feature of several neighborhoods (Hamid, 1992). Cocaine markets were relatively easy to enter, requiring a capital investment of only a few dollars to create a product with a seemingly endless demand (Fagan and Chin 1990, 1991). In the late 1980s, law enforcement officials characterized the crack industry as "capitalism gone mad" (New York Times 1989a 1989b).

Accordingly, the expansion of drug markets simplified the entry of women into drug selling. For women users, whose sales provided money and drugs, drug selling was facilitated by the expanded circles of users and the opportunities for selling. It was easy and cheap for women users to add cocaine and crack to the repertoire of drugs they used and traded socially. Their transition to drug selling simply extended their routine involvement in a variety of hustles such as fraud, larceny, and theft (Johnson et al. 1985; Hunt

1990; Murphy et al. 1991). For other women, drug selling was an extension of illegal careers and an opportunity for increasing their crime incomes. Reuter et al. (1990) and Hunt (1990) suggest that the retail cocaine markets were unregulated, comprised of many individual entrepreneurs who worked their own areas as they would a private business. Informal organizations formed along a freelance model where a small group of central players is surrounded by many short term employees who engage in dealing intermittently (Hunt 1990).

The decentralization and deregulation of drug selling removed many of the gender barriers to drug selling. However, to the extent to which the informal economy resembles the gender and stratification dynamics of the licit economy, women sellers continued to experience income differentials relative to males. And, they had more difficulty in reaching managerial positions or ownership of drug selling groups.

URBAN CHANGE AND STREET NETWORKS

The succession of drug "epidemics" over the last 20 years has mirrored a process of neighborhood disintegration and economic destabilization, both in New York and other inner cities (see, for example: Shannon 1986, regarding Racine, Wisconsin; Taylor, Taub and Peterson 1986 and Wilson 1987, regarding Chicago; Hagedorn 1988, regarding Milwaukee; and Sullivan 1989, 1991, regarding New York City). The drug crises have occurred in a context of rapidly changing neighborhoods where the formal and informal social controls that limited crime and governed drug use were weakened.

Beginning in the 1970s, the social and economic contexts of women's drug involvement changed extensively.[7] Shifting population composition destabilized social controls in poor urban neighborhoods. High rates of residential mobility followed the exodus of manufacturing jobs from cities. The concomitant exodus of middle class residents eroded informal social

---

[7] Since the early 1970s, neighborhoods and cities evidenced increasing social disorganization and isolation (Fernandez and Harris 1992; Tienda 1989a; Skogan 1990), intensifying racial segregation (Massey and Eggers 1990), rapid changes in population composition (Wilson 1991), and growing concentrations of poverty (Jargowsky and Bane 1991; Wacquant and Wilson 1989). Also, opportunities in the informal economy of barter, off-book labor, and unlicensed vending replaced the disappearing manufacturing economy during this period (Sassen 1989).

control mechanisms in poor neighborhoods as the middle class moved to better housing elsewhere in the city or suburbs (see, for example, Anderson 1990 and Wilson 1987). As these jobs disappeared, the ranks of unemployed adult males grew among those remaining in the increasingly poor inner cities (Kasarda 1989; Tienda 1989). Unemployment increased and wages decreased among Black males from 1970-90. This occurred despite a labor shortage economy (Freeman, 1991; Moss and Tilley 1991). As the relatively small population of heroin users aged out or desisted, new cocaine (powder, freebase and crack) initiation took place. This process occurred in a social context of increasing racial segregation, residential mobility, economic decline, and weakening social regulation.

The structural circumstances of women changed as well. Marriage rates declined (Mare and Winship 1991) and the percentage of female headed households (both with and without children) increased from 1970-80 (Jargowsky and Bane 1990, 1991). Stable employment rates among African American women in the same period masked important differences between poor and non-poor African American women. Employment for female African American high school dropouts and unmarried mothers declined sharply, while employment and wages increased for married women (Corcoran and Parrott 1992).

Since skills became a critical marker of employment success, manufacturing job losses excluded unskilled African American women from the workforce. The growth of the informal economy in New York City and other urban areas created both motivation and opportunity for unskilled women to participate in the legal and illegal informal enterprises (Sassen-Koob 1989). Throughout the 1980s, marriage rates, unmarried mothers' employment rates, and the real value of welfare benefits declined simultaneously (Corcoran and Parrott 1992; Farley 1988). Accordingly, and beginning in the 1970s, economic and social forces resulted in higher, more concentrated, and persistent poverty with adverse effects specifically for women. The growth of the informal economy in New York City, including an expanding drug economy, created both motivation and opportunity for unskilled women to participate in the legal and illegal informal enterprises (Sassen-Koob 1989).

For many young women in inner-city neighborhoods, economic marginalization was compounded by anxieties concerning their abilities to adequately fulfill the social roles of mother as well as consumer. These anxieties heightened during the past decade, in part, because of declining access to financial assistance and the failure of welfare payments to be indexed to inflation (Gans, 1995).

As neighborhoods grew poorer and younger, new female role models emerged to compete with the influences of "female old heads" (Anderson 1990). Alongside working women and women in "traditional" roles, the new "heads" displayed the "high life": buying fancy clothes, jewelry, drugs and alcohol, while eschewing marriage. Like her male counterpart, the "female old head" traditionally served as important community role models. These women believed in hard work, family life and "repeatedly and insistently told attentive boys and girls 'what was good for them'" (Anderson 1990:4). But as meaningful employment became increasingly scarce and drugs and crime became institutionalized in these poor neighborhoods, both male and female "old heads" lost their prestige and authority. With the expansion of the drug economy and its opportunities for "crazy money" (Williams 1989), street-smart girls (and boys) rejected the "old heads" lessons about life and the work ethic.

As family caretakers and role models disappeared or declined in influence, and as unemployment and poverty become more persistent, girls looking for direction to achieve a more conventional life had little direct personal support. The informal social controls of neighborhoods that helped to restrain female initiation into crime, particularly the traditional pattern of gender role socialization, in which the activities of girls were often monitored more carefully than those of boys (Hagan, Simpson & Gillis, 1987), eroded. Thus, changes in population composition and labor market access weakened the informal controls that regulated crime and drug networks and the people who participated in them.

THE CHANGING COMPOSITION OF THE INNER CITY

Nonetheless, in order to understand *women's* participation in these markets, two important trends regarding the disappearance of significant numbers of males from inner city neighborhoods need to be noted. For one, the risks of violent death or injury associated with drug selling resulted in a substantial increase in male mortality. Goldstein et al. (1989), for example, found that 32 percent of 414 homicide events in New York City were related primarily to crack sales. Similarly, the District of Columbia Police Department (Reuter, MacCoun & Murphy, 1990) estimates that 50-80 percent of the killings in recent years were drug-market related.

Second, the emergence of crack occurred in an era when crime control ideologies had shifted toward punishment, incapacitation, and retribution (Blumstein, Cohen, Martin, & Tonry, 1986). Policy responses to the spread of crack focused on street-level law enforcement efforts using mass arrests to sweep low-level dealers and steerers off the streets. Between 1980 and 1988, the number of drug arrests in New York City ((Belenko, Fagan & Chin, 1991)) increased from 18,521 (40% for heroin or other opiates) to 88,641 (44% for crack). Data on the criminal justice response to crack (Belenko, Fagan & Chin, 1991) suggest that crack arrests were being treated more seriously than other comparable drug cases. The results suggest further that New York City crack cases had a higher probability of pretrial detention, felony indictment, and jail sentence.

The end result was that persons, primarily Black and Latino men between the ages of 20-35 (Bureau of Justice, 1996), convicted of drug sales, especially of crack, constituted the largest proportion of all inmates entering jails and prisons in New York. Thus, the risk of being incarcerated or seriously injured as a result of participation in the drug trade was extremely high. Moreover, the high incidence of incarceration and homicide (Goldstein et al., 1989; Reuter, MacCoun & Murphy, 1990) among young, inner city, minority males, in the wake of the expanded demand for drugs, provided an opportunity structure for female entry into the informal drug economy.

The effects of these structural changes were evident in the street networks that shaped the social patterns of drug use, selling and crime. The guardianship functions of conventional institutions and of social networks were weakened with these structural change. The declining status of young men diminished their "gatekeeper" and mediating roles in both conventional and street networks in poor neighborhoods. Furthermore, young women were less likely to be involved in domestic arrangements or crime partnerships with males, and increasingly likely to be heads of households. To the extent that these contextual changes altered the gender composition and statuses of males and females in street networks, the mediating influence of street networks on women's drug and crime involvement was far weaker than among previous female cohorts.

Structural changes have brought increasing inequality into the economy and the lives of men and women who live in the most severely distressed communities. Three interrelated processes of capital disinvestment-residential segregation, racial inequality and concentration of poverty-have intensified the crime problem in these communities (Hagan, 1994). Economic dislocation has impaired the formation of social resources in distressed communities and families, weakening the guardian function of social networks, and indirectly encouraging subcultural adaptations to restricted opportunities.

It is not only the structure of opportunity that is distorted by the class transformation of the inner city. The social perception of this structure is altered, as well. Thus, it is not sufficient to recognize the importance of macrostructural constraints; it is imperative to understand the cultural significance of life in extreme poverty.

Because of experiences with extreme economic marginalization and social isolation in severely distressed neighborhoods, networks of kin, friends and associates tend to doubt that they can achieve approved societal goals. These self-doubts may exist either because of questions concerning their own capabilities or preparedness, or because they perceive severe restrictions imposed by a hostile environment (Wilson, 1991). The consequence, is lowered individual and collective feelings of efficacy.

So what develops and prevails within this shadow of low expectations is an attitude or code that places "respect" above all else (Anderson, 1994). In communities depleted of economic and social resources, some young women have attempted to gain respect or "recapitalize" (Hagan, 1994) their lives by investing in the value of public posturing, drug dealing and the use of violence.

Chapter 3

NEIGHBORHOOD, FAMILY AND SCHOOL

As we have argued, the structural and sociocultural changes of the past two decades influenced the development of women's careers in drug markets. As cocaine replaced heroin as the primary drug in street markets and as significant age-gender composition shifts occurred in inner cities, women became more extensively involved in drug selling than in previous drug eras. Women's roles and experiences in drug selling changed, from an adjunct selling-hustling role in deviant street networks to a more systematic and sometimes "high stakes" participation in drug selling. Thus, participation in drug dealing cannot be understood apart from the specific contexts in which it occurs. In this chapter, we will share with you the accounts given to us by these women. They will describe their neighborhoods, their experiences in schools, in their families, and among peers.

THE DISTRESSED COMMUNITY

Research on the community context of crime maintains that neighborhoods themselves directly influence behavior, attitudes, values, and opportunities (Bursik and Grasmick, 1993; Harrell and Peterson, 1992; Sampson and Lauritsen, 1994; Wilson, 1987). Community contexts shape what can be termed "cognitive landscapes" (Sampson and Lauritsen, 1994) regarding appropriate standards and expectations of conduct. That is, in severely distressed communities, a system of values emerges in which street offending is not vigorously condemned. For that matter, it often expected as a routine part of everyday life. These neighborhood structured perceptions and tolerances, in turn, influence the probability of involvement in illegal enterprises. But what were their neighborhoods like for the women we studied?

Like many other neighborhoods in New York City, Washington Heights in Manhattan and Bushwick, Brooklyn changed rapidly between 1960 and 1980. In Table 3.1, we provide data that are specific to these two communities. As you will see, by 1980, Washington Heights and Bushwick had become prototypes of what are referred to as "underclass," neighborhoods.

Washington Heights

Beginning in the mid-1800s, and continuing for a long time after, Washington Heights was home to German immigrants. During the 1930s, many Jews fleeing Nazi persecution also settled in Washington Heights, giving this neighborhood the nickname, Frankfurt-on-the-Hudson. The 1940s brought an influx of stable working class Blacks who left Harlem to settle into the brownstones and houses along Riverside Drive and Sugar Hill. And through the 1950s, working-class immigrant families from Ireland, Germany, Russia, and Poland dominated this neighborhood.

By 1960, Washington Heights had witnessed tremendous demographic changes. Germans accounted for only 16% of its residents. Instead, Puerto Rican and Dominican families, also working-class, moved in as White and Black residents who could afford to were moving to the suburbs. The non-Hispanic White population of Washington Heights declined by 32% from 1970-80, and another 10% from 1980-90. Hispanics replaced Whites at a 1:1 ratio during this period. By 1990, 41% of the documented residents of Washington Heights were Dominican and many more were illegal and therefore nonregistered immigrants from the Dominican Republic.

In large part due to the extremely high percentage of immigrants in the community, educational attainment for Washington Heights residents was low as compared to the rest of Manhattan and the other boroughs. Almost one out of every two adult residents did not have a high school education. Low levels of educational attainment were reflected in the types of jobs that were most common among residents: sales and technical support jobs, especially clerical work, followed by service occupations, and operators and laborers.

New York City's long economic recession and restructuring of the economy weakened, further, the labor market in Washington Heights. Many residents were displaced from light manufacturing, especially within the garment industry. They then found jobs only in the lower paying service sector (Duany, 1994). Many of these workers survived by selling food on the street, driving gypsy cabs or taking other temporary work in the informal economy.

It is important to note, too, that the unemployment rate over the past two decades was consistently higher in Washington Heights than in the rest of Manhattan or the other boroughs of New York City. Further, it continued to increase among residents, even as it began to decrease in the rest of New York. In 1970, 4 percent of the males and 5 percent of the females were unemployed. By 1980, the unemployment rate was 10% and 9%, respectively for males and females. And by 1990, official unemployment rose to over 13% each for males and females, a figure likely to be conservative in neighborhoods with concentrations of recent immigrants (Sassen-Koob, 1989).

In addition, during the period of 1970 to 1990, poverty grew and became more concentrated. The percentage of census tracts with 20% poverty rates rose from 13% in 1970 to 60.6% in 1980, and to 77% by 1990. By 1990, one in three Washington Heights residents lived in poverty.

During the 1980s, Washington Heights experienced a notable increase in female-headed families with children. Also during this period, the percentage of two-parent families decreased from 52 percent to 45 percent. Poverty was acute among female-headed families with children under 18. In 1970, 31% lived in poverty. By 1980, the percent rose to 59%. And, by 1990, we are able to see the real effects of the increasing concentration of poverty over this time period. For families with children under the age of five, 45% lived in poverty, and for female-headed families with children under 18, 64% lived in poverty. In 1990, at least 46% of Washington Heights children lived in poverty, compared to 36% in the rest of Manhattan and 30% city-wide.

Table 3.1 Neighborhood Social and Demographic Characteristics, 1970-1990

	Washington Heights			Bushwick		
	1970	1980	1990	1970	1980	1990
Population	180,710	179,941	198,192	136,770	108,605	119,240
AGE						
% 1-4 years	6.3	9.5	6.7	12.1	11.0	10.3
% 5-17 years	15.9	15.7	19.2	18.5	20.1	22.4
% 18-44 years	35.3	41.2	45.2	27.7	29.0	31.2
% 45 years and older	42.5	33.6	28.6	42.0	40.1	36.4
Ethnicity						
%Non-Hispanic White	60.3	28.7	18.8	35.5	15.6	5.7
%Non-Hispanic Black	12.7	14.5	11.5	27.9	26.4	25.1
%Hispanic	25.7	54.6	66.8	35.8	56.8	64.6
Employment						
%Unemployed males	4.3	9.7	13.0	5.6	15.2	15.8
%Unemployed females	5.0	8.6	13.8	8.0	14.3	16.4
Education						
%Persons 25+ with <High School Education	47.4	51.3	29.0	75.2	68.3	30.1
Family Composition						
% husband-wife	76.8	59.5	45.0	63.4	49.7	41.4
Poverty						
%Families below poverty	8.8	23.9	11.7	22.8	45.4	15.9
Concentration of Poverty						
%Census Tracts 20% Poverty	13.3	76.7	75.9	96.7	96.7	
	60.6					
%Census Tracts 40% Poverty	0.0	6.1	13.3	3.5	80.0	46.7
%Census Tracts Underclass	0.0	0.0	6.7	0.0	56.7	20.0

Sources: Kasarda, John, 1993. *Urban Underclass Data Base 1960-90*. Chapel Hill, NC: University of North Carolina.

New York City Department of City Planning, 1993. *Socioeconomic Profiles 1970-90*. New York: Department of Planning.

Amid these economic and social changes, drug dealing took hold in Washington Heights. It exploded with the introduction of crack in the mid-1980s. At about the same time, the streets of Washington Heights were besieged by violence. Homicides, many of which were drug-related, were clustered in Washington Heights.

People on the streets of Washington Heights were routinely exposed to the drug economy and violence even if they did not participate in it. For example, during one of our walks through the neighborhood, we noticed funeral wreaths and memorial candles in front of a brick building. It was obvious that someone had died there. Death appeared to be a regular visitor to this block. Painted on the side of the building was a black and gray mural of a cemetery. Listed on it were the names of the dead from the neighborhood, 51 in all. There was space for plenty more. As we crossed the street, youths leaning against the wall and asked if we wanted anything. Drugs, from crack to heroin, is what they had in mind.

Our short walk highlighted the grim realities of a neighborhood betrayed by the passage of time. Although most residents have nothing to do with drugs and violence, they were on the defensive. The drug dealers and street hustlers managed to set the tone for public life.

Bushwick

The 1960's were a time of rapid changes in the population of many neighborhoods in Brooklyn. In Bushwick, a large influx of Hispanics, mostly from Puerto Rico, began to displace the ethnic enclaves which had dominated the neighborhoods of northern Brooklyn. It was not until the 1970's and 80's that Dominicans and other Hispanics began to move there in large numbers. The percentage of Whites declined from 36% in 1970 to 16% in 1980 and to 6% in 1990, while the percentage of Latinos increased from 36% in 1970 to 57% in 1980 and to 65% in 1990.

"Blockbusting" activities by real estate speculators began the flight of Whites from Bushwick. Their exodus signaled the beginning of a long period of disinvestment, abandonment of buildings and high vacancy rates, arson, and drug-related crime. By the late 1970s, the process of ghettoization was nearly complete. The long period of devastation peaked in the 1977 New York City blackout, during which Bushwick was the most severely ravaged neighborhood in the entire City. By 1992, one-fifth of the zoned lots in Bushwick lay vacant.

Since the 1960's, Bushwick has been a relatively poor neighborhood (23% of families lived below the poverty line in 1970); by 1980, it was severely distressed. Nearly half (46%) of the families had incomes below the poverty level and 69% of female-headed households with children lived in poverty. Official unemployment rates among both males and females exceeded 15 percent by 1980, representing a 171% and 79% increase from 1970 for males and females, respectively.

The growing concentration of poverty in Bushwick was also reflected in the percentage of census tracts that meet each of three poverty definitions: at least 20% of the population below poverty, at least 40% of the population below poverty, and tracts defined as "underclass" (Ricketts and Sawhill 1988). For example, using the broadest definition of 20% population below poverty, Table 3.1 shows that poverty rose dramatically in the 1970s in Bushwick. Nearly all the Bushwick tracts had 20% of their population below poverty by 1980. The percentage of "underclass" census tracts, the most restrictive classification, rose from none in Bushwick in 1970 to over half (56.7%) in 1980, and remained at stable high rates in 1990.

Despite the relative homogeneity of the Hispanic population from the 1960's until the 1980's, they were unable to make any significant steps toward organizing themselves as a political force. Without legitimate forms of political power and representation within their reach, some Hispanics in Bushwick found that drug distribution was a route not only to wealth, but also to economic and political power.

Hilga, an old-time resident, noted that established distributors in Bushwick - 'owners' - possessed vast wealth and property within the neighborhood. They were clearly well integrated into the community. Her account of the first curbside distributor ended with the observation that he had built himself up from being nearly penniless to owning a 'fleet of cars' and many buildings in the neighborhood. She went on to describe how the area lacked many types of neighborhood organizations which existed in other parts of Brooklyn, and that many families were involved in the drug business.

> We never had any block associations. No, not in this neighborhood. This neighborhood wasn't together. One reason, I think, is because a lot of these people had a son or somebody bringing in some type of (illegally earned) money. Even *grandmothers* used to be lookouts. Whole families used to be

into selling drugs. Yeah, from the 70's on; when they started selling drugs in the streets, they needed lookouts. It was like a family affair.

Hilga's account suggests that the lack of participation in formal organizations among neighborhood residents was partially compensated for by the existence of family-based drug distribution networks. Additionally, she stated that these family-based organizations acted as springboards to political and economic power within the neighborhood.

Bushwick, like nearly every other neighborhood in northern Brooklyn during the 1960s and 1970s, had a variety of spots where local residents could purchase heroin, cocaine, marijuana, and other drugs. Many of these were indoor locations--bars, bodegas, pool halls, apartments. In these settings, a personal connection to the dealer was necessary in order to obtain access. Viva, a long time heroin user talks about the relative discreetness of street-level drug markets before the 1980s:

> At that time (1970s), they wouldn't sell drugs in the street too much. You would have to go like to a house. At that time there was Black and Spanish guys selling it. Years ago they used to sell drugs in a bar on Halsey Street. You go there, right, and they would sell to you. And then they had a house connection across the street from the bar. If they didn't know you they wouldn't sell. It's a lot different today. They'll sell to anybody.

Drugs sold outside during this period were mostly confined to public parks. There was virtually no trafficking on residential streets.

Though street-level drug markets had been present in Bushwick for many years, it was not until the mid-1980s that they began to expand dramatically and attract distributors and consumers from surrounding neighborhoods. This development should be viewed in light of city-wide changes in street-level drug markets during this period. Here, the process of market shrinkage in some neighborhoods led to the growth and intensification in others. Crack markets in central and northern Brooklyn generally began to shrink in 1988. The result of this overall shrinkage in Brooklyn crack markets was the emergence of an ethnically heterogeneous street-level drug supermarket in Bushwick.

By the late 1980s, there was a visible increase in the number of street-level distributors in the neighborhood. At the same time, there was an increase in the number of street-level drug users, many coming from other neighborhoods. These users would come to Bushwick in order to take advantage of the quality and greater availability of drugs in Bushwick as compared with other nearby neighborhoods.

Hope, a 43 year old African-American from Bedford-Stuyvesant offered us this account:

> Over here there was much more people, you know. Troutman is open all night long and stuff. It's like a 42nd street. My friend said there are some good drugs here. And I have to admit, the drugs were good.

By 1990, Bushwick was transformed into a mecca for drug distribution. Consequently, the use of violence was the currency of social control.

From these descriptions, a picture emerges of two severely distressed communities. In both settings, capital and public disinvestment processes made economic prospects bleak; community social networks and the social capacities of families was weakened; and crime became a short-term adaptive effort to enhance the lives of individuals and of communities. Yet, numbers do not capture how these women *perceived* the concentration effects of increasing impoverishment. During our interviews with these women, conversations turned to the neighborhoods in which they grew up. We were interested in getting their impressions of several facets of everyday life. We began with issues related to what Skogan calls "physical decay (1990)." In other words, we asked the women, "when visualizing the community in which you grew up what scenes come to mind?" For the vast majority of the women, they saw abandoned housing, rundown buildings and streets filled with trash.

These signs of physical disorder are important aspects of community life in that they "stigmatize it [the community] in the eyes of residents and outsiders alike" (Skogan, 1990:36), effecting morale and feelings of control. Further, they symbolize, in very concrete ways, society's disinvestment in this community. Abandoned and rundown housing, and erratic trash removal are all indications that local governments, landlords and business people do not see enough value to tear down or renovate the structures, open new housing units or businesses, and/or assure the health and safety of the residents by removing the trash. Instead, these buildings and garbage heaps are used for drug transactions and use, and as hangouts for the homeless, psychiatrically distressed, and for those engaged in "trouble."

In addition to physical disorder, the women recounted their childhood images of rampant "social disorder (Skogan, 1990)." Again, the vast majority of women remembered streets teaming with prostitutes, winos, junkies, delinquent youth and late night partiers. Most feared for their personal safety and recalled many instances when they observed their friends and neighbors getting hurt during street quarrels. They reported that muggings were a routine occurrence in their immediate neighborhoods, as were displays of weapons, which were often used in street fights. At least half of the women felt that homicides were *not* unusual and that theft and drug abuse were common.

Sonya, who grew up in Bushwick, provided us with the following description:

> Steppin' out of my building you would always see, uh, men cussing around the liquor store, drinking wine. There was always, uh, drugs in the neighborhood. It was dope. Mostly dope. I seen a lot of dope. I seen people layin' in the building after they been mugged. You know, blood and stuff around. I see people shooting up in the hallways. It was a lot of fightin' in the neighborhood too. Sure, violence and a lot of fightin' goin' on and cussin' and fightin' and cutting, lots of knives.
>
> I was always frightened. I was scared. And even when I ran with the gangs, I was, I was scared to death of guns. I remember playin' hookie one time in the park. We were drinking and this guy put the pistol to my head. I didn't know whether it was loaded or not. I just remember looking in the barrel, and I almost passed out. I almost past out I was so scared. When I was growing up it was important not to be an accident. A lot was goin' on. Kids gettin' shot accidentally, guys playin' with guns. And you just become a statistic. It was an accident, and I remember never wantin' to be an accident.
>
> When I was running the streets, I guess, I guess part of the thrill was an element of danger. I liked it. I liked it. And the time there was an element of danger, I was with it. But I still, I was scared, sure. But that, that, I guess that was part of the fun.

The disorder apparent in these neighborhoods was indicative of a decline in community self-control. Fear, demoralization and eventually resignation seemed characteristic of these women's responses to life in the neighborhoods. Denise nonchalantly describes life in Washington Heights:

> When I walked out of my house I saw a sick, depressing, ugly bunch of bullshit. I think it was somewhat safe in the daytime. At night it became ours, and you either knew how to deal or you didn't. You could get stuck up, you could get beat, you could get cut, you could get raped. Violence was everywhere. I was raped by three of my classmates. I was robbed twice. I've had black eyes, a fractured jaw. A knife was put to my throat. Drug dealing

was the pretty side. The pretty side. If you became a well-known drug dealer and you were good, you got the utmost respect.

These particular accounts of growing up in Bushwick and Washington Heights were not aberrations. They illustrate the visible reflections of the deep social and economic crises that were concentrated in these neighborhoods. In these neighborhoods, and in order to have some involvement in the "pretty side", young people, both men and women, became involved in a variety of serious and potentially lethal criminal activities. For many of these young people the standards of the "street code" (Anderson, 1994) were perceived as the only ways to gain respect and establish reputations. And, drug dealing was perceived as a real opportunity to succeed.

THE DISTRESSED FAMILY

Families exist as part of a **web** of social institutions that influence the behavior of members. As part of a network, families are affected by their access to a larger set of resources that provide economic, political and social opportunities and formal and informal behavioral controls. Many of these processes were described above as being part of the neighborhood context.

However, families also exert influence through their own set of processes that are related to and impacted upon by the broader structure. For example, families perform instrumental functions that provide for the health and welfare of their members. Thus, the extent to which a family has access to income, housing, food, health care and clothing, it is performing its instrumental function. Families also have expressive functions. Here, the extent to which the family fosters relationships of love and affection, emotional stability, a sense of belonging, self-esteem and dignity, it is performing its expressive functions. Furthermore, families tend towards being "decent", that is they "accept mainstream values and instill them in their children" (Anderson, 1994:82); or they are "street" in that they are "disorganized", self-destructive (e.g. addicted, violent) and socialize their children in the code of the streets (Anderson, 1994:83).

Unfortunately, families in neighborhoods such as those just described, are less likely to meet their instrumental or expressive functions and, at best, attempt to approximate "decent" families, but are more likely to be "street." Communities such as Washington Heights and Bushwick lack the necessary economic and political resources to generate socially approved of opportunities; and they are unable to cultivate the appropriate cultural controls to neutralize the attraction of illegitimate opportunities.

It is within this context that inner city families struggle to offset the draw to criminal behavior that pulls at their children. Unfortunately, many families fail. Their desperation and inability to manage the demands placed on them make it difficult for them to balance their own needs for control and catharsis with those of other family members (Anderson, 1994). As a result, children in "street" families grow up in families that are full of anger, frustration, aggression and deviance.

The women we interviewed, described a family environment in which there has been an overconcentration of various negative processes. For instance, 40% the women we interviewed reported that while growing up, they were *severely and regularly* beaten by a family member. This comes as no surprise since an association between high rates of child abuse and serious criminality, especially among the urban poor, has been found in previous research (Fagan and Wexler, 1987; Straus, et al, 1980)).

But the abuse was not limited to beatings. Thirty six percent (36%) of the women we spoke to were sexually abused by a member of their immediate family and 26% were sexually abused by someone in their extended family. These types of sexual assaults, that is between family members, especially when the victim is young, tend to produce the most trauma (Pipher, 1994:220). In addition, the resulting trauma is exacerbated when the victim feels she has no one to confide in, to turn for help, or no one who will provide her with support as she deals with his rage, resentment and anger. Unfortunately, the women in our study routinely reported that grew up in an environment in which they felt unprotected and alone in having to deal with the aftermath of abuse.

The distress experienced by family members and witnessed by the women did not end with abuse. Of the women with whom we spoke, 34% told us that during their childhood, they had at least one member of their immediate family who was hospitalized for a mental health reason. Typically, the patient was the respondent's mother or sister. Further, 69% of the women had a parent or sibling or had been arrested at some point while they were growing up. Many others reported family involvement in street crime, typically drug dealing, that did not end in an arrest. The presence of criminal behavior within the family unit provided these women with routine exposure to and socialization towards the tolerance of illegal behavior.

It should be noted, as well, that 72% of the women came from families with serious alcohol problems, and 86% lived with at least one member of their family who was drug addicted. One cannot underestimate the impact of drug and alcohol abuse on family processes. Studies have demonstrated a strong relationship between parental substance abuse and hostile family relations (Dunlap, 1992). And, research has pointed to the dissolution of protective family networks and practices as a result of such abuse (Anderson, 1990; Johnson et al., 1990; Dunlap, 1992; Loeber and Wikstrom, 1993). The disruption of positive family practices such as those just described has also been associated with high rates of crime and delinquency, especially violent offending (Sampson and Groves, 1989; Sampson, 1986; Felson and Cohen 1980; Felson, 1986).

Importantly, these women were growing up during a twenty year period of time, the mid-1960s to mid 1980s, when drug addiction took a terrible toll on their neighborhoods, exacerbating already deteriorating social, economic, and familial networks. Beginning with heroin and culminating with the most ravaging drug-crack- the already vulnerable communities, schools and families in which the women lived were racked by the effects of addiction. And, notably, the effects were most pronounced in Black and Hispanic families. The extended family networks that once acted to stave off disaster and provide for the instrumental and expressive needs of its members, were taxed by the ways in which addiction sucked at its lifeblood; and for Blacks and Hispanics, the result was a growing dissolution of these networks (Tucker and Mitchell-Kernan, 1995). Many children growing up at this time, especially those with addicted parents, had nowhere to turn for support and guidance. They experienced intense loneliness, difficulties in school (Sowder and Burt, 1980), and increasing isolation from conventional and prosocial activities. And, consistently they were warned to keep family "business" and problems to themselves.

You can hear the pain, rage and loneliness as the women we spoke to tell us their stories. Barbara, a Black woman who grew up in Bushwick during the 1960s and early 70s, recounts a life that was typical of the women with whom we spoke:

My mother and father lived together. But my mother was, uh, like the father and the mother. She was the strength of the house cause my father was an alcoholic. And, uh, he was just a little wimp. He was no help to my mother at all. All he did was cause a lot of trouble and heartaches. He's been arrested a few times, drunken driving, messing, fighting policemen.

Uh, the fact that my father was an alcoholic when I was growing up really didn't seem like anything was wrong with that cause most of the people I lived arounds fathers was alcoholics, or they didn't have a father in he family. So, it wasn't out of the ordinary.

My mother and father, they fought all of the time. As a matter of fact, my father tried to kill my mother with a knife. Even when I was real little I remember my mother having to hit my father in the head in order to stop him. My mother used to be afraid of my father. And there were times when she really had to stand up with him. At one time, he used to make broomsticks. They were called super broomsticks. And, she bopped him in the head with the super broomstick.

But she always would take him back, though. They would separate, and then she would take him back. And he would get drunk, and he would mess around with other women.

And, it would be unusual to open up the refrigerator and don't see beer or something inside, or people coming over on weekdays, uh, to have parties, and seeing people drunk and falling down and fights. You know it seemed too normal.

I also have three brothers and four sisters. My brother, Billy, he's been arrested--robbery on the trains, My sister's out there on the street. My baby brother does cocaine, crack and alcohol. The other brother is an alcoholic whether he wants to believe it or not. My brother Gary, too. My sister is a crack addict, an alcoholic, a garbage head. She's also been in a mental hospital.

My mother wasn't the type you could sit down and talk to. She always screamed and yelled about the things she wanted. There were times that I did want to go to her, but I was afraid because of her reaction. She didn't know how to really talk to her children. Whenever I would get in trouble or something, I wouldn't go to her.

But growing up like this wasn't so strange, it didn't seem so wrong cause most people had families like that.

Janelle provides us with a similar, although less vivid account:

My mother and grandmother raised me. I have one brother and one sister. Both of them are younger. I have lots of cousins. All of my cousins have been incarcerated, mostly for robbery. I used to be at my aunt's with them all of the time. I was also molested by most of my cousins as I was growing up.

My mother never said anything about my getting high because she drank herself.

I have one brother and one sister. We moved a lot but always to the same type of place. My parents lived together until I was 16 and then they tied the knot. Then they separated a year later and they never lived together again. And then my father died, a year after they separated.

My father was an alcoholic, and he smoked marijuana and he sniffed cocaine.

As hard as it is for most of us to believe, growing up in a household replete with domestic violence (physical and/or sexual), an alcoholic father, an emotionally absent mother, sibling criminality, substance abuse, and mental health problems was the norm for the women in our study. Take Monica's account of her family while growing up:

I have six sisters and two brothers. My brother Victor, my brother Freddie, my sister Anna, my sister Roma, my sister Mary were all arrested for guns, uh, drug sales, robberies. They have all been in prison.

My father used alcohol and my brother shot heroin, and my sisters drank---my mother used to sell reefer. My sister Doris was hospitalized for a nervous breakdown.

My family used violence all of the time. My parents threw things at each other, pushed, shoved, slapped, kicked and punched each other. They definitely beat each other. They even used weapons against each other. My mother to my father, my father to my mother. They used whips and a knife called a machete. Uh, and those little baseball bats. They're real small. They did all of these things to me too. My mother had these slippers that, uh, has nails stuck inside of them. And, uh, she had kicked back at me because I didn't sweep the bedroom. And the nails got stuck. I have a mark to this day on my leg.

My father sexually abused me. It first started when I was nine and he kept doing it. My mother knew.

By the time I was nine, I was in and out of foster homes because my father was physically abusing me. I never checked in with any of my foster parents about where I was going or what I was doing. I left when I was 15 because I was emancipated. I also lived in a group home where I got jumped by the other girls.

When I was 13, I was put in a mental hospital for unstable behavior. I was hitting myself, fighting. I mean I was just fighting all over the place. I actually did things to hurt myself. I tried to end it all by trying suicide.

Monica's view of her family, again, was typical of other women in our study. By and large, they viewed their parents as unable to love or be nurturing. Often, their parents' inadequacies were due to their own personal difficulties, including alcohol and drug abuse, unemployment, and mental health problems. Further, not only were many of the women exposed, as children, to their parents illegal use of drugs, but often to parental involvement in drug distribution. Here is Denise's description of her family:

> My mother and father were married. But he came and goes as he pleased. He was there a while, he was gone a while. But they basically stayed married. My mother was an alcoholic--valium taken behind the counter, shit. Valiums was my thing too. I got them everyday, them and a joint, and wine and anything else was Kool and Gang. It was all in my mother's house.
> My father was a laborer and he was also a drug dealer. Pretty busy guy. I found out one day at like a family dinner--a few of his friends, his colleagues. I asked him for like $100 and he said no, and I was furious. His friends said "You're not toasting your father?" And I said, "No." And he said, "Why not." And I said, "Which career am I toasting? The one in the day time, or the one at night?" That's all I said to him and he said go to your room. I said all right. I got upstairs, he flipped, I flipped, and I said I know what you do. I know how you pay for this shit. I know every fuckin' thing about you cause I'm out there. You fuckin' sell heroin, you sell crack, you sell dope, you sell wine, you sell every mother fuckin' thing. The only difference between you and Carlos and all of them is that they fuckin' stand on the corner and be real and you stand behind them and pull the fuckin' strings. He whipped my ass real good after this. His way of standing up to you was slapping you from here to there. But no matter how bad I was hurt, we could never go to the doctor because we couldn't let the neighbors know that.
> But I used to stick up my fathers' workers. And then he hired me to sell coke and dope. But, I was put in the Children's Shelter for vandalism and just some other shit.
> My uncle lived with us, too. He was like a constant felon. He was constantly in jail all the time for something-either it was stealin' on down to robbery back up to boosting and back down again. He taught me how to boost. He was an IV drug user. My uncle use to whip my ass. My father used to whup my ass and yell. My mother would try. My grandmother hit me, but she didn't mean it. They used cords, belts, extension cords, sticks, anything that they could get their hands on. Especially my uncle. He'd use anything he could get his hands on because he knew that if I got up, I was comin' at him too. After a while, ass whippin' was just not the move anymore.
> My father would curse my mother out. He would go upside her head. She would go upside his head. My uncle would beat up his wife. My grandmother was like, she would like just sit there like me and just chill. She went fuck it. I saw my uncle go raise his hand with a bottle to my

grandmother. And as he did it, I pulled out my pistol and I, boom, I shot the bottle out his hand. And I told him don't do that. That's my girl. Do not fuck with her. Ya'll can fuck with each other, and kill each other but don't fuck with her.

I was hospitalized, once. I had a terrible habit of like smashin' me against things. When I was angry, I would throw, break things and do it with my hands. They put me on an anti-depressant but I can't remember the name of it.

I felt my family didn't care. They didn't care. Sometimes my mom would ask where I was going. I'd say out mom. My grandmother would be the one to stand up to me. She would say you're doing this wrong. She found my razor and my pistol. She would take 'em. But I would tell my grandma that there's not really much you could do. I think my family needed to give a damn. I think they didn't need to be what they were. Now, I think they were like stupid.

The family's failure to perform their "guardian functions" (Sampson and Groves, 1989) and to socialize their children in terms of decency (Anderson, 1994) is clear from the above accounts. In addition, their inabilities were compromised even further by a strong mandate requiring that all personal matters, especially troubles, be kept to themselves. Thus, despite the lack of consideration they show family and community members, "street parents" do have a superficial concern that others view them as in control, especially of their children and their children's immediate environment. Therefore, when confronted with troubles, traumas, tragedies, upsets, disappointments, and victimizations, the women in our study were left to their own inner resources to cope. Under the best of circumstances, given their lives, the likelihood of dealing effectively with the types of problems these women would confront, was not good.

These families, incapable of providing protection and guidance also deprived the women of support that could have been given by members of their larger networks. Thus, the women were denied the benefits of guardianship but also those of "social resources" (Oliver, 1995) that may have helped them cope with their problems. L.G. shared with us her feelings of isolation. Despite the fact that her family was "intact", their own problems with employment, alcohol and drugs militated against their protecting and supporting L.G., especially after her rape. As she talks about her feelings of guilt and loneliness after the rape, she places it in the context of her family structure:

Uh, my stepfather was an alcoholic, and my mother was a Welfare recipient. In my family, one of the things my mother would always talk about to us is what goes on in the house stays in the house. And so I didn't have no way of ventilatin' or expressin' how I felt about what was going on at home; and my stepfather, who was an alcoholic, fought and beat on my mother. He would pull a knife on her. But she would take the knife from him and pull it on him. He would fight her and not give her money. And she was very dependent on him. I have a brother, too. When I was growing up, he was arrested for possession and sale. He's a drug user. Crack, dope, whatever. He's a garbage head. He's the one who turned me on to crack.

My mother, though, she was one of those women who would let you hang yourself, you know, give you enough rope to hang yourself. Even when I was raped I didn't go to her about it. I never told anybody about it. I never reported it. I think in the back of my mind that I had it coming to me. I had no one to tell me different. I couldn't tell anybody.

You know, to go out and do the things I did was influential...I mean influenced because I didn't have the family structure and help when I was growing up. So, a lot of the things I did, I knew were wrong.

Stephanie too described a family life bereft of support and bonds to conventional institutions. Her estrangement from positive social resources, like the school, eventually led her to a street gang and away from junior high school.

My mother and father were alcoholics. They was always drinkin'. My parents used to push and shove and beat each other. My dad knifed her in her mouth one time. He molested me and my sister. My mom used to beat me with an extension cord. She also used a curtain rod. I had whelps, I had bruises on my legs and stuff. I missed a lot of school. She kept me home from school so that no one knew about this stuff.

My sister and brother were crackheads. At 11 or 12, my mom started lettin' us drink. She didn't really try to make us go to school. By 15, this all seemed O.K. and I did and went what I wanted.

For the women with whom we spoke, the realities of life in "street families", were exacerbated by their marginalization from larger prosocial and guardian networks. Unlike earlier eras of inner city family life, these women did not have positive extended family relationships, involvement with a caring "old head" (Anderson, 1994:86), did not have a church affiliation, or attend settlement or afterschool programs. Further, as we will now see, they were estranged from school, as well.

Life in School

Generally, the research on childhood experiences in the confines of the school posits, at best a weak or indirect relationship with delinquency or criminal offending (Fagan, Piper and Moore, 1986; Jajoura, 1993; LaGrange and White, 1985). Furthermore, studies on the effect of dropping out of school on criminal involvement, too, are equivocal in terms of strength and direction of the association. There are some studies that indicate that dropping out has no direct effect on criminal involvement (Bachman, et al., 1978; Chavez, et al., 1989; Jajoura, 1993); or, that it actually reduces involvement (Elliot and Voss, 1974;or that it actually increases delinquent behavior (Thornberry, et al., 1985).

Our conversations with the women in our study fail to shed light on the direction or strength of these arguments. None of the women accounted for their involvement in street crime by stating that the conditions in school, such as boredom, discipline, or poor performance, caused them to cut class, drop out, or commit crimes to counter negative school experiences.

Nonetheless, during our discussions, it became clear that the school did provide a context in which larger processes were played out. Principally, there appeared to be the normal adolescent types of issues that were being performed in school. It is during adolescence that girls undergo a series of biological and social situations that require serious adjustments. And, it is during this time that girls act in ways to define themselves apart from their families of origin, are most vulnerable to peer pressure and, ironically, most in need of familial support. Even among the most stable girls, involvement in a variety of deviant behaviors is part of the *normal* adjustment processes (Pipher, 1994; Caspi, et al., n.d.; Stattin and Magnusson, 1990).

The school has been considered by some, as being an important context in which girls test out their responses to changes (Caspi, et al., n.d.). It is the social context in which opportunities for social interaction, self-evaluation and bonding occur. Further, it is one of the places where "youth who emerge from street oriented families...develop a decency orientation "{Anderson, 1994:86). However, it is also within the school context that deviant activities receive the greatest support, specifically by peers, not only in terms of initiation, but in terms of maintenance, too (Caspi, et al., n.d.).

It was in the school environment that many of these women met their delinquent peers. And, it was with these peers that these women engaged in truancy, vandalism, fighting, drug experimentation and other misbehaviors. Although we will save our discussion of peer effects on initiation into drug dealing for the next chapter, we do feel that a discussion of school experiences will set the stage for understanding what it was these women were doing while the rest of us were sitting in classes.

What were these women doing? Sixty-seven percent of the (67%) reported that by the age of 10, they were involved, regularly, in fights on school premises. By the age of 13, 89% were regularly truant, 26% regularly carried weapons with them to school, and 15% were involved in school vandalism. Further, it should be noted that the majority of the women in our study, 75% of them, dropped out before completing high school. In many ways, their disengagement from school was part of a larger process in which social bonds to other conventional institutions were being eroded. As the women decreased school attendance, the opportunities for positive socialization were attenuated.

However, from their accounts, a pattern of deviant and criminal behaviors was well established before their leaving school.

Here, Denise recounts her school days:

> I used to get into fights everyday. It must have started when I was seven. And, my mother was called everyday. We used to fight about anything--from you called me a name to I didn't like the way you looked. I'd fight with both boys and girls--it didn't make a difference. I didn't discriminate. You pushed me, I pushed you back.
>
> I started cutting classes, drinking and doing coke and reefer when I was about 13 or 14, in seventh grade. We used to blow up our lockers and other peoples lockers that we disliked. We used to do this for kicks.
>
> My friends were basically into the same things as I was. We used to cut classes and burglarize peoples houses, we would destroy shit, we would go to the park --a group of us five or six girls, we used to stick up couples. We'd grab the girlfriend, I'd hold razor. Guys are like apt to give you like whatever so you won't hurt his girl.
>
> By tenth grade this seemed more exciting and some of my other friends were dropping out, so I left to hang with them.

L.G. also dropped out of school to hang with her friends:

> One of the reasons I dropped out was, uh, hangin' out with the crowd and, you know, wantin' to be part of, um...just, you know, just a lot of wantin' to hang out with everybody else and cutting' a lot of tenth grade. We were experiencing drinkin beer and, you know, things like that. Smokin'

marijuana...we were doing things like that. And we'd fight. Girls went to scratch up each other's face and stuff like that.

I used to get into a lot of fights at school. Started when I was around eleven. I was like a school bully, you know. At first, I was one of those kids in public school who wouldn't fight back. And, you know, being a house of only two children, just my brother and I--he taught me to fight and, you know, I became very popular in school because I would fight back. You know, a lot of the children would look up to me and, you know, I was like the leader. You know, and I was a bully and, you know, I took advantage of people who wouldn't fight back that were just like myself at one time.

We also did a lot of graffiti. Started when I was 13. A lot of my activities were when I was 13. A lot of it stemmed from my home. You know, uh, a lot of the things that a lot of the other children had cause they had mothers and fathers who worked, uh, I didn't have. And, you know, wantin' a lot of nice things and wantin, to be part of the crowd, uh, drinkin' beers and bein' the bully allowed me to be part of it without having all the materialistic things that the other children had.

And then, by tenth grade, mostly all of us were dropping out of school.

In school, children act out their life experiences in interaction with others. Having witnessed aggression and violence in the home and realizing that the winner was always the one with greater physical skill, these women gained respect and self-esteem by practicing what they learned at home: "might makes right, and toughness is a virtue, while humility is not." (Anderson, 1994:86).

Jocorn, too, dropped out in tenth grade, but not until after she had established a career of fighting and street crime.

Yeah, I was a little involved in school, but I guess do to the fact that there's always arguments in the house with family members, and in the neighborhood I grew up in too, school wasn't so important. Basically, what I seen in my family and neighborhood is what I thought was O.K. and that was what I was taught--so who needed school. I figured, since I saw it at home and on the streets that gettin' high was O.K.. But, in school, I had a lot of problems.

I was nine when I first started fighting in school. With teachers, security guards. I was always short and I was always being bullied around. I didn't like being bullied around. So, I used to carry knives. One girl, I had a fight with 32 times. I counted them all. She came at me with a razor blade, right. She didn't like me. She was jealous of me, like, I had a lot of attention from the guys and stuff like that. She was like a bully at school, too. And, I had like a blade in my pocket. I wasn't sure what she was goin' to do. I just took it out and I felt somebody behind me So I just, I was scared, and I went and nipped her in the neck.

By the time I was 12, I was drinking and smoking reefer at school. I also did a lot of graffiti. My school friends were basically involved in drugs and burglaries. I was doing all of this to be a part of it, you know. I wanted to be accepted, to be part of a crowd. I wanted to be down with the friends, like they say.

Janelle dropped out of school in 11th grade:

Basically, you know, my friends...all of us played hookie. I wanted to be negative. I had a negative boyfriend, too. I started fighting, though, in elementary. I fought everyday. I wasn't getting enough attention at home. I would pull girls' hair, take their things, you know, like money, or, you know, like little keys, rings. You know how little girls come to school with little things to play with. I used to take them. And when they'd find out, we'd fight. When I was 13, I started caring razors with me to school. I was also doing a lot of drugs at that time. I'd used the razors sometimes when I was paranoid when I was high.

Alicia drifted in and out of school until she finally left in 11th grade.

You know, my mother used to drink a lot. I started drinking in school in 7th grade. I was always in classes for troubled kids. I used to fight a lot. I was a very violent kid. I used to beat my sister, and my mother was always beating me with an extension cord. So, I just started taking it out on the kids at school. I used to beat up the girls and take their money. I was wild in school. I started fighting in 4th grade and began carrying weapons when I was 15. I also started smokin' reefer then too. Living in Brooklyn and having a bad home life were two tough things to bring to school. I had a bad girl reputation at school. And, I had a couple of girlfriends in school who used to steal lunch money with me to get attention. Then, we started cuttin' school and robbin' people in the streets. That was also about the same time my stepfather used to molest me. My mother knew, but she was scared of him. He used to beat the hell out of her. You know, it was the environment. My mother was always calling me stupid, dodo bird. And, so, I thought that I was stupid. So, I finally left school in 11th grade.

By the time, these girls are adolescents, they have either internalized the normative orientations found in their homes and replicated in the schools, or they have, at least, decided that it was necessary to behave as if they did. These street orientations centered on presenting oneself as capable of taking care of business, of not needing anyone, of commanding respect. And, these street orientations filled the daily lives of the women while they were still attending school. But these women also recognized the precariousness of their positions and so were constantly on the look-out for threats to their reputations. Stealing others possessions, winning a fight, and perceiving each and every interaction as a potential threat to one's self-respect and reputation, circumscribed their school experiences. During our conversations about school, the women never spoke about the curriculum, their teachers, the administration or classroom interactions. Instead, their definitions of school days revealed their almost exclusive concern with finding their place in street life.

Chapter 4

INITIATION INTO AND THE CONTEXT OF DRUG DEALING

Despite the overwhelming concentration of economic and cultural impoverishment within inner city communities and families, as well as the ready availability of illegal opportunities, the majority of inner city youth avoid the pull towards criminality (Fagan, Piper and Moore, 1986). Clearly, the neighborhood, family and school environments, described in the preceding chapter, contribute to a general weakening in prosocial bonds. These institutions, with limited resources, a lack of cohesion and an inability to exert the traditional social controls associated with them, pale in comparison with the pulls of excitement, adventure, and belonging that peer involvement promise. And, it was within the context of weak family, school and community institutions and the *normal* course of adolescent development, that the women with whom we spoke, chose their peers.

The early stage of adolescence is fraught with many ambiguities that are wrought by biological, dispositional and contextual changes (Pipher, 1994; Caspi, et al., n.d.). It is beginning with adolescence that youth *normally* move from attachments to family to attachments to peers; it is when they *normally* experiment with drugs, alcohol and the sexuality; it is when they are *normally* most vulnerable to social labeling; and it is also when they are *normally* more in need of careful yet subtle support from their families and other neighborhood social institutions (Pipher, 1994).

Probably, we can all remember how, when we reached adolescence, our parents became openly concerned about the type of people who were our friends. Never before had they expressed such "interest" in our friends' grades, hobbies, interests, and other activities. Never before did they query us on how our friends felt about various situations. When confronted with an activity that our parents found problematic, the old rant and rave, "So, if your friends jumped of the Brooklyn Bridge (we both grew up in New York City), would you? became their war cry. (Okay, we admit to asking our own daughter who is now in early adolescence, if she would jump off the roof of the Beverly Center Mall, if her friends did).

But these parental worries, including our own, are not so far off from the concerns of contemporary criminologists. A substantial body of research has suggested that the more delinquent friends one has during adolescence, the more likely one will become delinquent him/herself (Agnew, 1991; Akers, et al., 1979; Elliot et al., 1985; Tittle, et al., 1986; Warr and Stafford, 1991).

The initiation and timing of entry into offending careers are key developmental life events and play a critical role in future social outcomes. Although the life course is dynamic in that developmental courses can be waylaid or rerouted, much research points to the importance of certain developmental issues, especially during early adolescence, that move children from having "conduct problems" to being initiated into criminality (White, 1992; Zucker, 1991).

Although it has been well established that peers play a critical role in the production of offending behavior, this research has been limited to understanding *male* initiation. A significant part of the literature on women and crime contends that women are "forced" into offending by males, drug addiction, victimization histories and the responsibilities of single parenthood (Arnold, 1990; Huling, 1991; Miller, 1986; Pollack-Byrne, 1990; Weisheit and Mahan, 1988). By and large, it is argued that domestic arrangements provide two important conduits through which women enter into criminal careers.

When offending begins early in a woman's life, childhood victimization is viewed as the main cause of female offending. Since between 50% and 80% of women surveyed in various correctional institutions in the country report being victims of domestic violence (Bureau of Justice, 1991), a direct, casual relationship is posited between "the experience of being victimized and subsequent offending" (Arnold, 1990). The chain of events leading to criminalization is then typically stated as beginning with child physical/sexual abuse, which produces a vicious cycle that includes running away, institutionalization, return to dysfunctional family unit, running away, and ultimately, street deviance (e.g., prostitution, drug use).

When initiation into offending occurs later in a woman's life, single parenthood is seen as another family-based pathway into offending. Given data documenting the large proportion of women offenders who are also mothers of young children, it is argued that women are driven into criminal activities by the responsibilities of single parenthood thrust upon them by the desertion of an uncaring and often abusive male partner (Douthat, 1988; Glick and Neto, 1977; Moss, 1986; Roman, 1990).

When pathways stray from home, drug use itself has been said to lead women into criminal careers (Arnold, 1990; Huling, 1991) The argument is that heavy involvement as an abuser reduces the options for women to engage in other income producing endeavors. Therefore, illegal activities provide women with opportunities to make enough money in order to buy drugs.

Notable for its absence in the literature on women's initiation into crime, however, is the possibility that initiation into offending, may, in fact, be linked to the same sets of processes as for males, especially in terms of the role that **peers** play in this dynamic. This prospect remains unexplored or is openly rejected (Daly and Chesney-Lind, 1988). Instead, women's introduction to street crime continues to be viewed in isolation from the larger context in which these women grow up and in which they **struggle** through adolescence, a normally difficult phase of the life course. Here, we explore the topic of female adolescents actually *choosing* to become involved with delinquent peers, who, by the way, are almost always females, and who engage in a wide range of street crimes, as well.

ENTRY INTO DEALING DURING ADOLESCENCE

Approximately 55% of the women in our study reported initiation into drug dealing during the earlier stage of adolescence, that is, between the ages of 12 and 15. Patterns of deviance were established during their early school years. For example, the women routinely cut school to have "hookie parties." And, it was during these parties, that these girls engaged in a range of behaviors that included shoplifting, burglaries, drug experimentation, and later, drug selling.

By early adolescence, these women had already been labeled as "negative" or "troubled" by school administrators. They exhibited a wide range of problem behaviors, consistent with what has been called "problem behavior syndrome in adolescence" (Jessor and Jessor, 1977). Some had been removed from the general student population and placed in special classes. Others officially remained on the school attendance rolls but rarely attended classes.

These girls, had, since elementary school, associated with peers who also engaged in problem behaviors. But, for these girls, peers seemed less to *influence* their behavior, but rather to reinforce earlier patterns that were established in interaction with family members, usually, brothers, sisters or cousins. This does not come as a total surprise. Recently, there has been a growing body of research that has explored the role that siblings (and by extension, extended family members, e.g. cousins) play in influencing the development of deviant conduct (Rowe and Gulley, 1992). This may be due to several factors: (1) the lifestyles of siblings create opportunities for deviant involvement (Rowe and Gulley, 1992); (2) emotional attachment between siblings may produce greater behavioral resemblance-- a greater willingness to model behavior after each other (Rowe and Gulley, 1992); or (3) sibling conflict may produce more generalized patterns of aggressivity (Patterson, 1984 cited in Rowe and Gulley).

Here, Monica tells us of her family's influence:

> Oh, yeah, my two brothers and six sisters all were very close. They were older than me. When I was a little kid, my brother Victor and brother Freddie, along with my sister Anna and my sister Roma and my sister Mary were all into robberies, guns and later drug sales. My father was an alcoholic, my brother shot heroin, my mother sold reefer. My sister Doris was the only one not into it. She had a nervous breakdown. I used to love to hang out with them. They were always talking about how exciting their stuff was and sometimes, especially, when I got to be about 10 or 11, they would let me come along with them.
>
> Then, when I got older, maybe 12 or 13, I went out on my own with my friends. I hung with people who had talents. We'd make a little bomb kind of like thing and put them in police officer's cars like the little cars that looked like mail trucks. And, we'd drink and sometimes meet my brothers and sisters and hang with them.
>
> Oh, yeah, around that time, we started smokin' reefer--me and my girlfriends. They would just pass the joint around and I'd take. I just took it. Then when I was about 14, I was hangin'out with a crowd that smoked angel

dust. At fifteen, I started gettin' into ludes [methaquaalone], but just on weekends. These were things we just did on the side--sort of to party.

In Monica's case, as with many of the others, sibling (in some other cases, cousin) effects on her deviant behavior preceded, and were then reinforced by her involvement with delinquent peers. This familial resemblance, may be due to the influence of a "moderator" factor (Baron and Kenny, 1986 cited in Rowe and Gulley), such as neighborhood and/ or family distress that preconditions these behaviors, rendering these women "deviance prone" (Zucker, 1991).

On the other hand, 35% of the women we interviewed were not involved in drug dealing or other criminal behaviors until the latter years of adolescence, from age 15 on. Take for instance, the case of Stacie, for instance,

> Until I was 15, I was really involved in school. My brothers and I were in the Boys Club. That was a real positive thing. From the Boys Club we got involved in a lot of activities. We got into swimming, and, uh, we got into a lot of little talent things. We did some, uh, traveling with the Boys Club for tournaments and Ruckers, you know, we went to shows and things. It was really good for my brothers and me.
> Everything started when I was about 15. The kids I was hangin' with outside of school were a pretty wild crowd. It was great. I could get really get loose with them. We'd smoke marijuana, cut out of school, write our names on walls--we wanted to be out there. We'd fight other groups of kids.
> At the beginning, I led a double life. I was doing really well in school. My friends in school were all "A" students and into sports. And, when I was home, I cleaned the house and helped my brothers and sisters with their homework. When I was home and when I was in school, I just did everything positive. When I was with my friends outside of school, I did everything negative. I was really attracted to negativity. Then I started hangin' with them more because the attraction was so strong. They had pistols and knives and they got into mugging. I guess this part of the thrill of being there--the fact that there was an element of danger. I liked it. I liked it. It was part of the fun. Then we all got into LSD, angel dust, powdered cocaine and stuff. We would drink and get high and then go to the park. I would do anything they wanted to do. I wanted to be accepted by them, they were fun. They didn't make me go out mugging with them, but I wanted to. It wasn't really peer pressure, but there was a feeling that I had to do it if I really wanted to be accepted.

For later onset girls like Stacey, peers played a more direct role in their initiation into drug dealing and street offending. Furthermore, unlike the early onset group, drugs were much more central to their interactions. For this later onset group, initiation occurred because of situational pressure to jointly participate in what was primarily a social behavior.

The transition from "positive" peer interactions to ones that were "negative" did not appear to be drastic. The gradual replacement of prosocial peers with delinquent ones occurred over a one to two year period of time, during the middle stages of adolescents. For that matter, the women in the later onset group recalled holding on to their prosocial friends for quite a while before either leaving them to join their delinquent peers full-time; sometimes though, their positive peers began to shun them. As April recounts:

> I used to have two groups of friends. One group, the positive one, I had been in since elementary school. The other group was always getting into trouble. I began to hang with this crowd when I was 15--to fit in. And I began to like it because it made me feel like I was important. My friends who were always doing everything right tried telling me, uh, what I'm doing, I'm doing wrong and stuff like that. Some of them shied away from me a bit. As time went on, I let go.
>
> I started drinkin' when I was 15 and I was doin' it regularly. And when I would meet people they would lead me to the progression of the drugs and that's what I did. My first crowd was into drinking and smoking pot. And then I met another crowd that was into cocaine. Both groups were all girls. I did that for a while and I kin' of grew out of that. Then a girl friend introduced me to crack. I liked that a lot better. I didn't like to be drunk so I didn't really like alcohol. I didn't like reefer because I felt I couldn't function. I didn't like cocaine because of the way it affected my nose, my nostrils. And the crack seemed like, you know, it felt like it made me more alert.

For Stephanie, the pathway was quite similar:

> Everything really started when I was 15. I was actually doing OK in school. But at that age, I had, I don't know, I had a need to be with friends and let go. My friends were all from school. I had two groups of friends that I worked with. One was positive and the other was negative.
>
> My positive friends knew I was hanging with the others but it really didn't matter to them. Sometimes they would say you better not go there. Like when it was coming down to playing hookie, it was like either go to school with this group or play hookie wit the other. When I would play hookie, they would help me out by giving me the things I missed in school and the homework.

> When I was hanging out with the others, we was doin, shoplifting, drinking wine and smokin' marijuana. The shopliftin' was for the excitement that became in the blood after a while. You know, I really got high off of getting over in stores and things; and many times I had plenty of money in my pocket and I would still go and steal things. I got a lot of attention from these friends, from my shopliftin' Even though it was negative attention. We then got into drug dealing, burglaries and robberies. That was when I was about 16.
>
> My parents didn't know about my runnin' around. I lied, I kept secrets. They only knew my positive friends. When they found out about the others and tried to keep me in the house, I was defiant. I stayed out. They gave up.

For the women in the later onset group, peer initiation into offending, brought with it a change in how they interacted with their parents. They reported an increase in lying to their parents about their out-of-school whereabouts and in sneaking out of their parents' apartments in order to join friends. At precisely the point when these girls needed parental supervision and support in order to overcome the pull towards street life, the parents gave up. Some parents locked their daughters out of the house after curfew, others heightened their physical responses and yet other parents sent their daughters away--to live in foster care, to live with a neighbor, or to a psychiatric hospital. In all of these cases, the types and levels of parental supervision of their daughters' behaviors changed, and like their male counterparts, these girls began to spend more time away from home, in unstructured activities, with peers and becoming more heavily involved in street life.

Regardless of the age of onset, by the ages of 16 or 17 the overwhelming majority of these girls had permanently dropped out of school. Their relative independence from parental and school controls gave way to the importance of their peers as direct influences on street deviance. And, given the neighborhood context, the opportunities for such activities were abundant.

Drug use for these women further expanded their repertoire of street activities. It increased their contact with entrenched members of local drug markets--users and sellers--and, it expanded their opportunities to participate in both these roles. Until the point of addiction, though, drug use for this group of women remained ancillary to their involvement in a more generalized lifestyle on the street that included a wide variety of criminal activities. However, once addicted, drugs played an important role in amplifying the involvement of these women in drug dealing, to a large extent, in order to support drug habits.

This was the case for Alicia:

> We'd been together since we were 12. We'd be stealin' from other kids--a couple of girlfriends of mine and me. I just wanted to be a part of it. We used to buy cigarettes, beers, you know. And that's when Boone's Farm was out. But it was the fun of robbin' that was what got us.
>
> And then it progressed. When I was 15, I started payin' more attention to robbin' people in the streets, you know- not just other kids. I liked it. It was really exciting. I started takin' blotter, drinking a bit more. I liked the high life. I liked hangin' out with my friends and everything.
>
> By the time, I was 16 or so, I wanted to get down and sellin' seemed one way. I started hangin' more with the people who sold us drugs. First, I started selling opium, then reefer. Then around 17, I started selling dope in Bushwick, my neighborhood. After a while, though, I was bringin' in $800 a week just from dealing. I still did some robbin' with my friends--just for old times. Then, we'd buy some stuff, sit around and get high. Then, I got into free basin'. I started gettin' into the life. By 17, I was hangin' out all night, free basin' and selling, sleepin' all day. I got into the night life.

Unlike other adolescents, these women's involvement in problematic and experimental behaviors did not recede in late adolescence. For that matter, by their accounts, their involvement in drug markets and other antisocial conduct *increased* as they entered young adulthood. Instead, the excitement, calm and pleasure they experienced as a result of the pharmacological effects of their drugs, combined with their increasing marginalization from prosocial activities and deeper involvement with deviant peers, drove them further into street life.

INITIATION INTO DEALING AS A CONSEQUENCE OF DRUG USE

For serious drug users, "becoming an occasional dealer is almost an inevitable consequence of becoming a competent regular user" (Faupel and Klockers, 1987, p. 60). Many of the women in our study (63%) became dealers to support or subsidize their personal drug use. For Stephanie and Evelyn, "taking care of business" (Preble and Casey, 1969), was both a hustling, moneymaking enterprise and an intrinsic part of their social world of drug abuse. Their accounts exemplify the transition from drug user to drug dealer.

Stephanie: Well, when you're out there, and you smoke crack, you know who has the best. You know who buys. I mean you know who you buyin' the best from. So when you become a very steady, reliable customer because you're coming every day. If you're a crackhead, you're there every day, you get to know these people. You talk to them. You know, you bring them more business.

They begin to see you and trust you. So then you can work for them one day. And they know that when you come to them and say you want to work, it's because you want to take care of your own needs.

Evelyn also entered dealing through her drug connections:

What happen was I didn't have any money, I didn't have any way of getting a job, I was already addicted into crack. Like I said, my parents threw me out of the house, there was no way means of getting any money from them or anything like that, I had bumped into people who were selling, and I got connected with them two spots selling drugs with their bosses. I said, I can help you out, be your look out or whatever, and from there I started working and I met the bosses and I started working like that.

Whoopi was initially reluctant to sell drugs but her increasing crack use left her with few options.

I started selling crack by me wanting to smoke. And a lot guys telling me, a lot of guys use to tell me, Yo Whoopi, Why don't you sell. And I use to say, people use to offer me, all...I use to say, I was like this, I am not selling.

Yea, my mom wasn't going for me bringing that shit into the house. But see I was open with her, I was telling her, what I did. You know what I was doing. She's like don't bring them in here. You know, don't bring them in here. But the only one who came in here was Dereck. He lives on the 8th Floor. I use to help him, Because I use to see, all the bottles all the time I use to smoke, I use to keep my little bottles, accumulate bottles, anybody who needed bottles, Yo, go pick Whoopi, cause she got bottles. All colors, any color, any size, and you know what I am saying. I had your white, orange, red, green, black, blue, purple, yellow, I had every bottle you needed.

You know what I am saying, they say, Hey Whoop, get me some bottles. I'd say, how many do you need. They'd say, how many do you got? I'd say, how many do you need? They'd say 100. BOOM. I'd give them 250. You know what I am saying? And I'd give them two or three bottles. Two or three bottles for myself, off of you know what I'm saying.

One day Dereck said I need someone that is going to be in the lobby and work. See, since you'll be in the hallway and you know everybody, hey its there. You know. I was smoking a lot, needed money. So I took a couple bundles and sold them. I made straight up money. It was easy money.

If we pay careful attention to these accounts, it becomes clear that the transition from user to dealer was a common process. Given the neighborhood context in which these women were socialized, it was not unusual to find that dealing was a normative part of the overlapping social networks in which these women participated. As we have argued, these women were members of distinct communities that mediated between them and the larger economic and political organization. It is within their local communities that the women interacted and made decisions regarding school, work and family. And, it is within these local communities that they devised ways of coping with the demands imposed by the larger structures. Community levels of family dysfunction, economic and social dislocation as well as the presence of illegitimate opportunity structures provided the landscape for the lifestyles and routine activities which were related to the women's participation in drug dealing.

Darlene describes the terrain of drug dealing: the violence, the profits, and the ease of entry:

> The building I lived in, they were selling on the fifth floor. Uh, I seen a young lady get beat down with a gun, the butt of a gun for going over the limit. I seen shootouts. I seen guys that I work for ride up on somebody and shoot them for owin' them money or, you know, tryin' to set them up, that type of stuff. Again, when you live in that, like, kind of neighborhood where I was running the streets in, you see a lot of that. You figure like this it's not you, and you leave it alone.
>
> So, the guy asked me if I wouldn't mind working one day. You know, like he told me how much he'd pay me and how much drugs I would have. It was no problem. It was like, I grew up in the sense with dealing. I knew what it was all about. Like so many people around me was dealing. I said to myself, damn this life is exciting.

Some of the women (16%) began drug selling as apprentices, typically in social settings where lovers, family members and/or friends also were dealers. Their social networks, however, included mixed sex groups where there was little evidence of social processes mediated by males in dominant roles. In part, this reflected the fluidity of their relationships with males, including intimate partners, and also the importance of female friendships in their everyday lives. Sonya and Hernimia tell how male partnerships facilitated, but did not control their selling activities:

> Sonya: I started selling crack and dope when I was 23. I was dealing with (a known drug kingpin). I was a runner. ... A lot of women coming up now, especially younger teenage girls, they're involved with young guys who are drug dealers, their women are going to get involved with it. That's what happened to me. Because I didn't always want to ask him for money to support me I had to go out and do it on my own. So I used his connects to put me on my feet.
>
> Hernimia: I started to hang out with this guy. he use to deal crack. And, we just like became like partners. Uh, he would give me like the merchandise and I would sell it. I've been into it for like, yeah, about seven years. But see, I never stood like on a corner and sold like bags or anything like that. It would always be quantity. I has like a few customers, four or five customers. Me and my partners sold ounces. He was like one of my suppliers.

Hernimia goes on to describe the involvement of her father in the business:

> When my father came out (prison), I started like working with him. He had sold pot and heroin with my uncle. I worked with him for about 1 1/2 years. He was my last partner.

Earlier studies suggest that initiation of women to drug selling was often mediated by men (Waldorf 1973; Rosenbaum 1981; Anglin, Hser and McGlothlin 1987; Waterston 1993). Frequently, prostitution often was a context for this initiation (see, for example: Goldstein 1979). These views tended to portray women as passive accomplices to male drug use and dealing, void of the same-sex friendships that were the contexts for male initiation, and launching a process of immersion and engulfment in the man's social networks.

As we see from the above accounts, the women sellers we interviewed showed little of the passive vulnerability in entering drug sales that characterized women in earlier, primarily heroin, drug eras. For the women we interviewed, becoming a drug dealer was an opportunistic extension of their life experiences (Mieczkowski, 1994). Essentially all of the women were already participating in quasi-criminal lifestyles (e.g., drug use, shoplifting, fraud, robbery). Driven by choice, necessity, or a combination of both, to be independent, to survive, led to the decision that, like many other hustles, drug dealing was an excellent way to "get over." In this regard the women reflected a choice pattern that was quite similar to previous studies of males.

Another mode of entry into dealing entailed the expansion of an existing product line (Murphy et al., 1991). A number of women (21%) started selling such drugs as marijuana and heroin and learned many of the aspects of dealing before they moved on to cocaine and crack. These women already had developed selling skills and established a network of active customers for illicit drugs. Denise described how she came to expand her product line:

> I was still running my business, my old business; but it wasn't lucrative enough, cause people weren't... there wasn't a whole lot of dope... it was like crack then. So I got turned on to it. I had to look at it like well how can I like turn this into money. And, uh, this old man from Manhattan came out and taught me how. He taught me how to cook up coke, how to bottle it, and how to, how to sell it.
>
> Yeah, we bought powder, and cooked it up. And for a little while, for the first month or so, I only made like, just about $1,000. Just enough to re-up. And that wasn't good enough for me. I put the word out that I had quality. Before I knew it I was sellin'... I was makin' $6,500 per week if not better. Then I got workers. I had workers in the street and at night I had another house that they'd work out of, uh, as long as I paid the girl's rent which is only $250. They sold out of her house. I had ten people that worked for me. I had four runners. Four muscles, very strong and very capable men. Myself and to people that sat in the house. Except for the muscle, all the others were women. Girls I went to school with. Girls I trusted. Girls I did shit with.

Denise and her workers quickly learned that crack selling rates (number of transactions) were far higher than the selling rates for other drugs. Clearly, the dynamic nature of the crack market and its profitability contributed to the immersion of women into selling roles. And, this immersion also enjoined them to the social networks of crack selling.

Initiation into crack use also accelerated the career trajectories of the women in our study. The women's own drug use expanded to include crack while at the same time, it produced little dropoff in the use of other drugs. This suggests a even deeper involvement in drug markets and in social networks of users and sellers. At the same time, it suggests a further weakening of ties to conventional activities and people.

ORGANIZATIONAL ROLES

Like other businesses, cocaine selling is hierarchically organized with higher incomes concentrated among a small number of managers. The bulk of drug workers labor for hourly wages and, occasionally, drugs. They are drawn from the vast surplus of laborers who either lack the human capital to be successful in legal work, or who voluntarily leave low paying and unpleasant jobs for what they perceive as the higher incomes of drug work (Bourgois 1989; Waterston 1993). Our women sellers did manage to achieve roles in distribution that were different from the support roles that typified their involvement in heroin selling. The roles suggest an active involvement in selling that required handling money or drugs in direct selling transactions. Most (98%) were involved in direct sales either in curbside or indoor locations, a relatively rare role in the heroin markets of the 1970s (Johnson et al. 1985).

The following accounts epitomize the typical selling experiences of the women:

> April: Sometimes I, I would be up two or three days in a row because the money would be coming so fast that I'd be, I wouldn't want to go to sleep because I knew if I would go to sleep, I would miss money. On a typical day, I would wake up in the morning. Somebody would probably wake me up wanting to buy drugs and that was how my day started. They would call or beep me, and, uh, from then I would be on the run all day. And sometimes my run would last two or three days. Uh, I used drugs to keep me motivated, to keep me moving. And I felt powerful.

> Darlene: Madness, pure madness! You wake up, you know. You be behind a, a steel door-- workin' from under the door. Me, I would smoke crack first. I seen a good thousand people a day, you know. Maybe the same people over and over, but about a thousand people a day.

> L.G.: A typical day would be wake up, uh, take the first hit, get wide open and begin selling--all day into the night. Sometimes into the next morning till 3, 4, or 5 in the morning. It would be pretty busy on Friday and Saturday nights- Thursdays too. Sunday morning the crack business would be booming--people coming constantly. Working people, people coming all times of night, all night long until they're dead broke. Yeah, it's sad, but that's the way it is.

In general, the women had several different roles. In addition, they often occupied more than one role at any one time. Some (42.0%) had management roles that involved "supervising" other sellers, distributing drugs for resale, or collecting money. A significant number of the women (53%) were involved in important roles such as "scale boys" who weighed and distributed packages of cocaine powder for street sales. Others provided more service-oriented roles including "steering", that is, directing users to a dealer. Patricia spoke about her relationships with her "customers":

Table 4.1: Drug Selling Roles and Patterns

	N	Percentage
Dealing Roles		
Street sales	153	98
Steering	113	72
Lookout	102	65
Manufacturing drug products	.83	53
Manager/Crew Boss	65	42
Buying in large quantities	67	43
Selling drug paraphernalia	65	42
Dealing Organizational		
Sold alone	25	16
Sold in a group	127	84
Characteristics of dealing groups		
Had a specific name	46	30
Had a specific boss	126	83
Had rules & sanctions	122	80
Had specific territory	125	82

Percentage of group members reporting each feature.

> The main way I make money is takin' people to go cop drugs. I got maybe eight or nine different customers. They are mostly White people from Long Island who can't afford to get busted or they're too clean cut to go on the block or they're scared to death to go on the block. Usually, I would cop a bundle or better. Dope, coke, both. When they come from Long Island they

don't come down here to buy less than a bundle. A bundle of each. That's 150 dollars. Usually, I'll get a bag of dope, a bag of coke and twenty dollars.

Most of them are older than me [34]. Most of them are 40s, 38, somewhere around there. They mostly have good jobs. They all got their own houses. All of them have nice cars. There's two of them who take the train, but they do have a house out in Long Island.

I have one female customer from Long Island used to be a top, top supervisor with Sony's, you know, top name TV brand. I mean, I'm talkin about top dollars. Sometimes she comes twice a week. Sometimes she comes once a week. She buys two bundles of dope and two bundles of coke. She gets off up here. Sometimes she buys syringes from me, but if I don't have any I'll go to M___ and I get it from him. She'll buy four or five at a time. She hooks it up in the gallery. She gives me a shot from it. She gives me my own one and one. But she needs me to hit her though. I'll hit her in her arm. She can't hit herself at all. I'll hit her before I do any drugs.

Few of the women (9%) in this sample were "owners" of drug groups or "queen pins." In part, the ethnic and family segmentation of the drug labor market made it difficult for women to achieve higher ranks. The retail drug trade in Washington Heights, for example, was dominated by immigrants and first generation Americans from Latin American countries. They either were tied through kinship networks or knew each other from their country of origin (Williams 1992; Waterston 1993). In these organizations, women were seen as ill-equipped to handle the violence that was necessary to maintain security and control. These perceptions justified the assignment of women to lower paying jobs such as line workers (baggers, for example) or other support roles that did not involve the handling of large quantities of drugs or cash.

Nonetheless, the expansion of drug markets in the cocaine economy provided new ways for women to escape their limited roles, statuses and incomes in previous eras. The emergence of women sellers earning high incomes suggests a new dimension to women's drug involvement. Denise's account illustrates the varied entrepreneurial skills involved in running and maintaining a drug organization: how to keep books, pay bills, manage inventory and cash flow, calculate profit margins, and deal with competitors and unpredictable employees and customers:

I would get up a seven. I would work out, have breakfast, shower, decide what I'm gonna wear--call all around to see who got what. Everybody was meetin' at my house to count out money and we'd have a little coffee, a little small brunch, count out money and see where everybody's at. Then I'd have to make a run. But before that I went down to my closet where I kept the files on who's short and how often. Then, on my way out, I would stop and give the kids in the neighborhood $10. I'd sit up on my little fuckin' Benz and I'd talk shit to the niggers all day and play the radio and maybe go for a ride. If it was a day when someone had been short 4 or 5 times, then I'd have to take care of them. If they smokin' my stuff, I take care of them. I whoop their fuckin' ass and I'm cuttin' their shit up. Same goes for rival dealers--I 'd go shoot your shit up I'd go tear your place up. I'd stick up your workers. I'd cut up their clothes. I'd take your shit and I'd do it everyday until you either moved or you came to work for me. I like nines. I like Barringers with nickel plated handles. I like style and something that works well. A woman can catch a bad one if she ain't prepared. I have rules--don't steal from me--ask me for something and I'll given it to you but don't steal from me. I have this one West Indian girl and I pay her $750 plus anything she want to eat. If she saw an outfit she wanted, she got it. She never skimmed from me and she never took from me neither. When all's done, I settle in and smoke-- about $1000/day. That's a typical day, on a rampage, I smoke more.

The explosion of crack use fundamentally altered fundamentally the structure of dealing networks from primarily a confederation of free-lance sellers and dealers (i.e., in which all parties work without clear status distinctions on an as-needed or temporary basis) to vertically organized dealing groups (Johnson et al., 1990). That is, the crack trade was a market of numerous entrepreneurial sellers who had to employ role-specific employees to consolidate their business- enforcers, guards, hawkers, supervisors of street sellers-all of whom may have been assigned a particular location.

Although women's roles in selling were different from previous eras, the diffusion of drug markets in the cocaine economy complicates any comparisons with heroin or other drug markets. But like the previous eras, women generally were at the lower ranks of the drug business. They tended to occupy the more service-oriented roles played at the street-level of dealing: "steering" (directing users to a dealer), "touting" (acting as an advertiser for a dealer) and "selling."

Many women sold in mixed sex organizations, organizations that provided them with basic services such as mutual security from robbery, market share, and easy access to product for selling. Sometimes, the selling organization was not just an economic context, but a social world where identities were formed while incomes rose sharply.

MAKING AND SPENDING MONEY

For the women with whom we spoke, incomes from dealing rose significantly over time. Furthermore, their average weekly incomes from dealing were substantial, hovering around $5,280. The women's expenditures, though, changed commensurate with their increased incomes. But, incomes rose faster than did expenses. Although actual expenses on food, clothing and shelter changed little, their percent share of overall expenses declined. The primary increase in expenditures, both in dollars and percentage was for drugs. Expenses on drugs rose from 30 percent to 65 percent of total expenses. Whether for personal consumption or resale, increased incomes were allocated to drugs. This focus of economic life on drugs was further evidence of the social embeddedness of women in street networks organized around drugs, as well as their isolation from conventional social and economic interactions.

What becomes of the marginal income? It is neither saved nor invested in conventional ways. The women's accounts of monetary exchanges suggest that excess earnings were dispersed through family and social networks, as well as through consumption and conspicuous spending. Money was given away to family members in the form of food or purchases of household goods, or gifts to loved ones or girl/boyfriends of cash, jewelry or clothing. Older matriarchs of intergenerational families frequently were the recipients of this largesse. These financial contributions were often rewards or signs of recognition for the support and care that matriarchs and siblings provided for these women's children. A good deal of excess earnings were spent conspicuously on lavish gifts or goods (cars, clothing, jewelry) or expensive entertainment. Regardless of how the money was spent, the women recognized that their access to excess cash was likely to be temporary. Wanda described what she did with money, and how she evaluated the options of drug selling and licit work given her human capital:

> I made $2500 a day. I spent it on jewelry and clothes. I had everything I needed or wanted. I wasn't't getting high. The organization didn't want us getting high. A lot of women worked for the organization. What else can we women go out and do to make money that don't need a college degree. You need a high school education to scrub toilets. But I decided that I was going to enjoy

my money before it was over. No way I was going to get more like this.

DEALING AND VIOLENCE

Nonetheless, involvement in crack distribution markets did not come without significant risks.

> I got shot in my head. They tried to rob me for my coat. This was two days after Christmas, right here in my head. Now I was coming from, you know, the back of this building where I deal, it was dark. I was going to the store, and these two dudes came up to me and grabbed me for my coat. One of them tried to grab my coat from the collar, and I see this shining gun so I tries to grab it and it went off on my head. (Val)

Violence has been viewed as an *intrinsic* feature of all drug distribution markets. In historical studies of illegal opium and alcohol markets (Musto, 1990; Zahn, 1989) as well as in empirical analyses of marijuana (Adler, 1985), heroin (Goldstein, et al., 1984; Johnson, et al., 1985) and crack (Dembo, Watts and Wright, 1990; Fagan and Chin, 1990; Goldstein, et al., 1987; Inciardi, 1990; Williams, 1989) markets, belief in the drugs-violence association has remained strong. Further, research on the crack-violent crime connection suggests that the crack-cocaine market itself produced a direct and dramatic increase in violent and often fatal offending (de La Rosa, 1990; Goldstein, et al., 1989; Johnson, et al., 1990; Lambert and Gropper, 1990; Hamid, 1990; Schuster, 1990; Sterk and Elifson, 1990).

The tendency towards the routine use of violence became especially prominent with the expansion of crack markets. In the absence of any legitimate authority, violence was used to settle disputes and enforce discipline and boundaries. This relationship between drugs and violence has been observed in literally hundreds of empirical studies. People who use and sell drugs are more likely to engage in violence than non-drug involved individuals. Accordingly, although women generally have low base rates of violence (Sommers and Baskin 1992), their entry into drug use or selling increased the risks of violence.

As Goldstein (1985) has suggested, there are three ways that drugs and violence are related to each other: 1) the pharmacological effects of the drug on the user induces violent behavior, 2) the high cost of drug use impels users to commit economic compulsive violent crime to support continued drug use, and 3) violence as a common feature of the drug distribution system, which he calls systemic violence, serves a variety of purposes. Violence in this context is used to protect or expand drug distribution market share or and/or it used to retaliate against market participants who violate the rules that govern transactions. As the following accounts indicate, the system of drug use and distribution created a structure of situations conducive to retaliatory violence.

Sonya spoke of her use of violence to protect her drug dealing turf:

> I was involved in a lot of violence, a lot of physical violence. Sometimes I used weapons, a gun, a knife, with me it didn't matter, anything in my hand was a weapon. Somebody would get in my territory, I'd shoot at them and tell them to get off the corner, you know, that's how it was generally done. It became too much for me to handle alone, so I incorporated my boyfriend into my crew. Sometimes we had weapons. Usually women don't like to be known selling drugs so sometimes they have a male front. There are a lot of women drug dealers. They have males to front off for them, to keep the attention off of them. You have to have some type of protection over yourself. A man who they believe is the boss.

Stephanie described the necessity for violence as self-defense:

> I was selling up and down the block and these two guys went to rip me off. Right, they both approached me, and they kept askin' me what I had. I told them what I had. They kept sayin' let me see, let me see, like they were gonna take whatever I showed them, and I wouldn't. So I was grabbed from behind, and the guy that was standing in front of me, he grabbed my collar. And, I was already high and paranoid. And I slashed him. I slashed him with a razor. When I slashed him, his blood shot out. The other guy released me. There was blood everywhere. They let me go. Because of the sight of blood. And then most people didn't expect that type of thing from a person like me. That's why they tried.

Evelyn's use of violence was for the purpose of social control:

> Well, there was this one girl. I had...it was coincidence, I happened to meet up with her here. I had taught her, ya know, cause she was selling drugs and the guys used to take advantage of her and I didn't like that. I despised

that. So I took her home with me and I told her 'Look, this is what you're gonna do.' And I was teaching her well. One day she went out and it was something she wasn't doing. She wasn't getting high. She came to me and she was $40 short of my money. And I asked her, 'Where is my money?' She said, 'Ma look. I was hangin out and they stole my money.' And I got angry with her because of the fact that they played her out for her money. It wasn't't that fact that she was short the $40, because I always give her more than that to take home. It was that fact that she let another crackhead come and play her out, when she should know their game. That's exactly why I bust her ass. Because I wanted her to learn.

Fights with buyers and sellers over bad drugs, and robberies of buyers and dealers were the most prevalent forms of systemic violence. Val described an incident over buying bad drugs:

One time, one time, I went uptown, to get some, I went to this spot all the time, what happen was, my man that I always get it from, wasn't there. When I say my man I mean the regular dude that I buy it from, not my man. So we went down this block, to this other kid, it was like three o'clock in the morning. He sold us the wrong kind of blow. He sold us some sniff and blow. Sniff and blow, you can't do like that. You can't cook that, cuz it dissolves. We waste a lot of money. We spent a G that night. Three o'clock in the morning we go all the way back to Staten Island, cuz we had a cab, try to cook it up, and all our shit was just fucked up. You know we was mad. Me and my old man. So we went back up there, got strapped. This was 3:30, now this was all through the same time in the morning. Boom they was gone. So we came up there the next day. Now mind you, I sell drugs outside everyday, So customers be looking for me. So imagine how much money I lost with in them four days going back and, still take me straight to the forth day. We's caught up with them and shot one sucker the others ran and got away.

Rhonda tells a similar story:

I made it my power. If you fuck with me, I am going to screw you. You know. The one guy did owe me some money. This guy, right, I knew he had top notch shit. One Sunday morning, I was thirsty. I went to Jimmy, I said, Jimmy man, you got some. I said bags. I bought two bags with my last $20. Get back home, the shit was bullshit. I went back to Jimmy, what the fuck is this? I went up in the guys face and said I want my mother-fucking money. He jumped back in my face and I cut the mother-fucker. I said don't sell me that shit again. Cause I'll stomp your face and ruin your rep.

Workin' Hard for the Money: The Social and Economic Lives of... 69

At times, violent interactions were an outgrowth of neighborhood resistance to drug dealing. Barbara described one incident with a neighbor:

> I was selling drugs in Manhattan, out of an apartment building. I was going downstairs when this guy says what are you doing here? He starts hassling me and pushes me. He says 'we don't wants drugs in this building.' I never saw him before. He seemed high. I saw he had a knife in his hand. I had a .25 caliber. I was shot at twice while selling and I was robbed once. They were users. I always carry a .25. I shot him in the shoulder.

Overall, twenty-six percent of the women were involved in systemic violence. Victimization, however, was more likely violent a experience than it was commission of a violent act. Close to half (46%) of the women were victims of crime in the course of drug transactions. Rose described an incident:

> Yeah, I was working and selling all day, see I was, like I said, when I first started free-basing I wasn't in it all heavy, it was just like, maybe after I worked I would buy like $50 worth, and go home and smoke it and after that just go to bed. I use to make a lot of money when I use to sell dust. Like, maybe, thirteen or fourteen hundred dollars a day. People that observed and that be out there scheming on things like that knew. And one night I was on my way home and I was living with my sister, I was walking through a building, I was going to this crack spot, pick me up some and go home. And um, these guys stopped me, it was 3 of them. They had the hats on with the eyes, I didn't really know what at the time was going to happen. They asked me if they could have a light, and I said no. And the other one grabbed me and said you do so and pulled out a gun on me. And I said I don't got nothing and I start to fight, and the guy hit me on the mouth with the end of it. And blood started gushing and I lost my teeth. It was hanging over, it was so big. And then I started getting frighten and they made me take off my clothes right in the middle of it, you know. And um, went all through my pockets, and cuz I had money all over, my shoes, my socks, my pants pocket, and shirt and I had a leather bomber I had bought. And I had cut the pocket and puts my money all in my coat. And I had it with the pockets, it just doesn't feel like it was cut all around. You just put your hands in the pocket. The guys were going to take my clothes, and I said please don't take my clothes, you got the money so just go, you know. So I guess they felt sorry enough, and left the clothes, and they ran and I put back on my clothes back on and I still had money in my coat, you know.

Interpersonal violence also occurred within the system of drug use. Alicia talked about one incident:

> At age 17 I caught a case, attempted murder. It was dealing with drugs. We were hanging out and this guy got high over some angel dust. He flipped on me and we got into a fight. But he was tripping and he and he was really trying to hurt me and I wind up stabbing him. It happened at his house. One minute everything was OK. The next minute, everything was all going crazy. He attacked me with a knife and I grabbed the knife and I wound up hitting it away from him and I stabbed him and he died.

It is clear from the accounts provided by the women in our study that interactions between victim and offender and sometimes even the interaction (verbal) of a third party played a fundamental role in assault incidents. These women were not roaming willy-nilly through the streets engaging in "unprovoked" violence. Frequently, they were thrust into violence prone situations. Often, the victim entered into it as an active participant, sharing the actor's role and becoming functionally responsible for it. Thus, in addition to Wolfgang's examples of victim-precipitation those cases in which "the victim was the first to show and use deadly weapon" or "to strike a blow in an altercation" (1958, p:252), the present data suggest that the victim was functionally responsible for a great many more types of motivating behavior. The offender's conduct may have been a result of open and direct provocation; it may have been the outcome of an opportunity produced by the existence of the victim; or it may have emerged in relation to the demands of the victim.

The violence found in drug selling has been interpreted in one of two major ways. On the one hand, it is viewed as an economic behavior in that it regulates market relations. Thus, as a social control mechanism, violence in drug selling attempts to control competition among rival dealers, assure the quality of goods and services, discipline the work force, and protect the participants from hostile elements within that environment.

On the other hand, the violence that is associated with drug market participation has been explained as being more generic. In other words, it has been found to exist as part of a more generalized pattern of crime and violent behavior that permeates the neighborhood at large. Thus, the drug distribution market is viewed as just another domain of community life that is fraught with violence.

The present data, as well as other research (Fagan and Chin, 1990; Johnson, Williams, Dei, and Sanabria, 1990), suggest a more symbiotic relationship between drug markets and the communities in which they exist. Violence among drug sellers, including females, appears to reflect the concurrence of two processes: the self-selection of people who routinely use violence in their broader social and economic interactions and, the neighborhood itself, in which violence is taught, practiced and maintained as a way of negotiating the social realities of street and domestic life. Consequently, it is not the drug business, itself, that makes people violent. Nor, are people violent in the context of drug selling, alone. Rather, drug selling provides a subcontext that sustains the use of violence within a larger social setting where violence is used more generally.

In addition, it has been suggested by others that participation in drug markets and/or violent offending as well as the risk of victimization are all linked by more generalized aspects of lifestyle and patterns of behavior (Fagan and Chin, 1990: Sommers and Baskin, 1993). Further, it has been demonstrated that these patterns exist independent of major demographic and individual level correlates of criminality such as gender (Jensen and Brownfield, 1986; Lauritsen, Sampson and Laub, 1991). The current data indicate clearly that the lifestyles and routines engaged in by the study women increased the probability of their exposure to situations that were potentially violent as all as increased their risk for personal victimization.

Chapter 5

LEGAL AND ILLEGAL WORK: WORK, CRIME AND DRUG DEALING

The sharp rise in drug trafficking that characterized many inner cities during the 1980s and early 1990s has often been associated with a precipitous decline in formal employment opportunities. This "disappearance of work" (Wilson, 1996) has been seen as altering the basic calculus used by young people to influence their choice of economic activities. By and large, the outcome of such decision-making, in the context of dwindling wages and satisfactory job opportunities in the legal world of work, has been increased participation in illegal income generating activities (Fagan, 1992; Freeman, 1983; Hagedorn, 1994; Witte and Tauchen, 1994).

In recent years, research based on this model of decision-making has flourished. Elements of the economic calculus have been dissected and results supporting the choice of crime *over* legal work have been reported. Increasing unemployment and underemployment have been identified as significantly related to crime participation (Chiricos, 1987; Blackburn, Boom and Freeman, 1990; Tilly and Moss, 1991; Corcoran and Parrott, 1992; Fagan and Freeman, 1994); income from crime, especially from drug dealing, has been found to be higher than income from other, legal sources (Vicusi, 1986; Reuter, MacCoun and Murphy, 1990; Fagan 1992, 1994; Freeman, 1992; Wilson and Abrahamse, 1992); and the social and psychic payoffs from illegal work seem to outweigh the concern over, if not the risks of legal sanctions (Fagan, 1996). Thus, the choice of illegal work is understandable, at least, intellectually.

Once the decision to enter the world of illegal enterprise has been made, another body of research has sought to explain the persistence of illicit income generation activities. But again, the research has focused on males' experiences. Ethnographic studies, for instance, have documented a renouncement of the secondary labor market by inner city males. Young males who have turned to the illegal economy now rely on street networks for status (Anderson, 1990, 1994; Hagedorn, 1988; Padilla, 1992, 1993; Taylor, 1990; and Moore; 1992a, 1992b). And, they use the discourse of work, like "getting paid, or " "going to work" (Sullivan, 1989) to describe their criminal careers. Thus, for these young males, money from crime, and reputation from criminal success form the bases for commodity consumption and status that would be unavailable to them from the legal workaday world.

Further, research indicates that once involved in criminal careers, young males in the inner city perceive that entry into the world of legal work is unlikely. At this stage of criminal career development, research points to the rise of a rigid bifurcation between licit and illicit economic activities (Anderson, 1990, 1994; Hagedorn, 1988; 1994; Taylor, 1990; Moore, 1992). Thus, young males eventually choose to *either* abandon their involvement in illegal work and accept the economic and social parameters of the conventional workaday world, or they commit themselves to illegal work and its concomitant social and legal implications. However, once the decision to commit to the illicit economy is made, the option to return to the licit world is narrowed, if not eliminated altogether (Hagan, 1994). This bifurcation has become, if not an empirical reality, one that at least characterizes much thinking in this area.

Other research, however, suggests that participation in the *worlds* of work may not be exclusive. In fact, several studies show a much more dynamic and flexible interaction between legal and illegal work. Some qualitative studies have documented regular career "shifts" from illegal to legal sources of income and even simultaneous participation in both economies over the course of an individual's work history (Shover, 1985; Biernacki, 1986, Sullivan, 1989, Padilla, 1992; Adler, 1992).

In this chapter, we explore how the women in our study progressed from early involvement in the legal and formal economy, their joint involvement in these two spheres and their ultimate embeddedness in the informal and illicit economy. Through a description of their experiences in these various "work" sectors, the women provide us with an understanding of the bases for and types of decisions they made when choosing their "vocations."

It is clear from their accounts that even from the outset, a tension always existed between their involvement in legal and illegal work and between the asocial world of formal labor and the seemingly social atmosphere promised by criminal involvement. Further, we find that the "economic" calculus so often reported in the literature is only partially the basis for their decision-making; and that their maintenance in these criminal activities comes to resemble less the workaday world described in relation to male criminal careers and more like the world of drug addicts, that the traditional literature on females and crime suggests.

PARTICIPATION IN THE SECONDARY LABOR MARKET

For the women we interviewed, legal employment was viewed as important, at least initially. By the time they were sixteen, the majority had left school. Therefore, securing a job took on great significance. And, at least at first, they were successful. Unlike their male counterparts, most of whom experienced high rates of joblessness from the start (Wilson, 1996), 83% of the women we interviewed were able to secure employment in the formal economy. These jobs were exclusively in the secondary labor market.

Of the women who worked, the vast majority were employed in entry level, unskilled positions as office clerks, factory laborers and salespeople. Some of the women were able to obtain "aide" positions in home health care or education. These positions were acquired either through temporary employment agencies or public programs, never through personal networks. They lasted no more than a few months and were characteristically low paying, offered little long term security and no chances for advancement.

The women in our study entered the labor force with an acute awareness that their employment, even in the future, would, in all probability, be sporadic or remain in the lowest echelons of the secondary market. For the majority of the women, then, aspirations regarding employment were low. And, for the few women who hoped for more lucrative futures in the licit job sector, training in cosmetology and having their own "station" at the local beauty salon was their loftiest goal. But, even at the outset, these women did not think that the jobs available to them would bring the "prestige, pride and self-respect" (Liebow, 1967:60) found in white collar occupations.

The work descriptions offered by the women we interviewed confirmed this perspective. Furthermore, like the men Liebow described and those studied by Bourgois (1995), the women eventually came to view these jobs with an active disinterest. They were routinely fired due to excessive absenteeism or were absent frequently as a way of quitting. They would often show up for work high on drugs, or coming down from a night of heavy drinking and partying. Often, especially towards the end of their involvement in the formal economy, they used their work environments as settings for their increasingly prevalent criminal activities, particularly, drug distribution.

THE INTERMINGLING OF LICIT AND ILLICIT WORK

At the beginning of their employment careers, the women attempted to make a living, primarily through legitimate employment. Over time, however, they decided that the low economic and cultural returns from their marginal employment were not satisfactory. They then turned to crime and illegal hustles for supplementation. For many women, the workplace itself came to serve as a setting for these activities. And, it was these activities that provided them with important sources of income, identity, and excitement.

Here Monica, a former summer youth worker, describes how she combined licit and illicit work to augment her desires for more money, more excitement, and the respect of her peers on the street:

> I started as a summer youth worker for a City agency. But then they kept me permanently as a floater, which means like I worked diversified duties. I worked with administration, receptionist, advertising-I did all of that. I made, like, $9,000 a year. At this point I was already indulging in cocaine and I started selling drugs. So, uh, I started going to work and showing people my material-people that I knew that got high. And they started buying from me. So then they started buying weight which would mean that I would have to get more material-and give it to them. And, uh, where, also it's like I used the messenger companies from the office. I used to call the messenger companies, and they used to pick everything up. And they would come pick it up at the agency and drop it off at someone else not knowing what was really inside. I made like $4000 to $5200 a week. It depends because I was still shopping for a lot of weight. I just wanted more money, and I just

wanted to have my own-not work anymore, and travel. But then I just started using all the money for getting high and I stopped going to the office.

Maria, too, used her place of employment for her illegal enterprises.

> I got involved, not to live on, cuz I made enough money from my job. It was just extra money. To do other things.
> I would go, where-ever I wanted to go. Just extra money, like one of those Miami trips, you know, Puerto Rico trips.
> It was in demand. I just had a friend that was right there in town. I didn't have to go far. So I used to buy in large quantities and sell to people from work. I knew who were into drugs, I would, you know, let them know when I had something for them. And they would, would get from me right then and there. And this went on during the course of the day. I cleared about $500 to $700 a week.

Other women recounted for us incredible work schedules in which, for the majority of the time that they were employed in the legal sector, they would also hold down "second jobs" during their off hours. For these women, an overarching addiction to drugs pushed them to secure money by any means possible--legal *and* otherwise. April was one such woman:

> I was makin' like $7 an hour at this Sears job. That was actually pretty good money, but I was gettin' high. I was stealin', robbin', I used to forge checks to get more money. I worked there for maybe six months. I guess I was into fast money, a fast life. I needed money to support my habit. It was no way I could support my habit workin' on a job. So I needed money. So I went out, and, uh, the person that I was buying from, I asked him, you know, how can I get into it.
> So, after I was done with my day at Sears, I was selling on the street. I turned out to be one of the carriers- the person that, uh, pick up the drugs and distribute it to people on the street to sell. I bring in about $2000 to $3000 a week. Sometimes I, I would be up two or three days in a row because the money would be coming so fast that I'd be, I wouldn't want to go to sleep because I knew if I would go to sleep, I would miss money--the Sears money and the other--I wanted both.

For the drug addicted women, losing sleep, being absent from legal work, partying, and hustling formed their day to day experiences. For these women, crime on the side was a continuation of their long term involvement in offending. Initially, it counterbalanced the asocial and boring nature of their jobs in the legal sector. It provided these women with the excitement, adventure and comraderie absent from jobs in the secondary labor market. Further, and not unimportantly, drug dealing supplemented the meager incomes they received from their marginal jobs.

As L.G. recounts:

> When I was like 15-when I dropped out of school after, you know, a lot of places weren't taking people that didn't have a high school diploma and stuff like that-I went to a temporary agency, you know, which allowed me to work for different companies. I did clerical work for the Department of Probation. I did clerical work for AT&T and Citibank. I worked six or seven months in each of these places. Usually the job itself had ended and I'd go back to the agency and they place me again. But they were all boring--no one to talk to, to hang out with, but I kept going. But even though I was workin' and still doin', you know, the right thing, I always was drawn to doin' the wrong thing somewhere down the line.
>
> When I'd get home from work, I'd go hang out with my friends. We got hooked up with some people who were, uh, transportin' drugs from New York to New Jersey to Washington, and I started doin' that for a while after work, on weekends, or between jobs. I would get paid large sums of money and I, you know, I clung to that for a while. But I was really into for the fun and for things to do with my friends. I did like the real money, though.
>
> But then I got mixed up with harder drugs. I went further down and stopped going to the temp agency. Smokin' crack was like, just all I wanted to do. So, I sold crack for a percentage, just to have some to smoke, I would sell. I would sell for drugs and collect welfare.

L.G. was socialized initially into drug dealing primarily for non-pecuniary reasons. The money she received at the early stages of her dealing career was secondary to the excitement and adventure she received from her participation. However, as L.G. and her counterparts entered their late teens and experienced a desire for a more sustained source of income, they applied the criminal "skills" learned earlier, to more economically motivated activities. But, even within this context, noneconomic motives were still important. For these women, dealing with friends and enjoying the fruits together were still meaningful.

Nonetheless, once addicted to harder drugs, i.e., crack cocaine, L.G. and most of the women in this study, experienced the ultimate rupture in ties to the licit workaday world and a decline in the importance of excitement, adventure and peer participation in criminal activities. Thus, drug addiction and not peers came to organize most of daily life's activities.

COMMITMENT TO THE ILLEGAL ECONOMY

Patterns of dealing varied among the women. As we have heard, some abandoned work after periods of licit employment, others drifted in and out of legal work while firmly committed to drug distribution markets. Herminia's account was typical of this latter group of women:

> I had lots of little jobs, but selling cocaine was always how I really made my living. My last job was, I was 18, I was a receptionist at a showroom. I was there maybe one year. It was okay. But I was already into selling cocaine. I started that much earlier when my father went to jail. I knew my father was selling coke, but my father didn't know that I knew. I don't know for how long he was doin' it, and I realized that the money that was comin' into the house, into my mother's house, was coming from selling coke. And I felt that as my duty as taking care of my family I started selling coke. My father didn't know anything about it at first. But there came a time when we were doin' it together. We were selling together.
>
> Now, I'd be selling for about seven years. I went up and down. I could make $500. I could make $3000 a week. It depended. I never stood on the corner and sold bags or anything like that. It would always be quantity. I had a few customers, four or five customers. I was selling ounces with some Colombians. They became like my suppliers and stuff. I started like with myself, when my father came out I started like working with him. Then I stopped working in offices altogether.

Other women from the outset considered the illegal economy as their primary job commitment. They chose *exclusive* "careers" in crime, principally dealing, and never participated in the secondary labor market. For these women, given the alternatives of low-wage payoffs from legal work and the expectation of relatively high returns from income-generating criminal activities, they viewed dealing as a rational choice not unlike choices made among legitimate occupational pursuits (Fagan, 1994).

Jocorn and Rose both had a rich history of pre and early adolescent involvement in violence, crime, and drug dealing. For them, by the time they reached their mid teens, hustling was a way of life. As Rose recalls:

> Like I said, I use to live in a neighborhood full of hustlers. And um, they use to watch me go to school, giving me $5 or $10 buy clothes off the street for all the kids in the neighborhood. And then just, we started hanging down there by them. Then we started holding drugs for them. And paying us, $100 a day, and we would hold a 100 quarters, now if I would have gotten caught

with that, lord knows how much time, but I was too naive and young to know what was going on. The money was good to me. I thought I was rich, you know what I am saying. And I liked to buy. So, by the time I left school, I was already into my job on the streets. I knew how to do the job and I had no problem protecting myself while I was doing it.

Jocorn, too, was deeply entrenched in her "career" by the time she left school. And, she stayed in this one "job", advancing through the ranks until she had her own organization.

> I was about eleven or twelve when I started selling drugs. I'd sell reefer, valiums, acid, syringes. It was fast money. I guess that's what attracted me to it, the fast money and the fun. I was makin' about $500 a week. Much later on, when I was about 17, I started like putting people to work for me. I was pulling in $10,000 a day. I'd moved to selling dope. I found with dope, like I had customers that would come from Boston to buy for $10 and sell them up there for $30. When I found this out, then I had people go out there and sell it. Then I got more money.
> I sold it all. Crack too. I've been dealing for 19 years. The more I had, you know, the more money I wanted. I had people in Brooklyn, Manhattan, the Bronx, Boston, in upstate. All I was basically doing was gettin' the drugs and receiving the money.

The "career" trajectories of the women in the above accounts reflect the influences of structure and context in shaping their choices and options. With limited access to legal work, and in segregated neighborhoods with high concentrations of joblessness, alienated views of legal work and diminished expectations for conventional employment became normative. For some of the women, the criminal involvement of family, friends, and neighbors were more likely to integrate them into the criminal world than into referral networks for legal employment. For others, immersion in crime during childhood and early adolescence marginalized them early on from interest in or access to job contacts in the licit workaday world.

But, for those women who had some experience in the secondary labor market, commitment to criminal careers eventually ended their involvement in legal work. Denise told us about her break with marginal labor:

> But there was more money to be made. About when I was 20, I started to sell drugs with my father and uncle. I made about $1500 a day! Well, see, $500 goes back into the business, and clothes, hotels, men, friends. I dealt heroin for about two years. Then I went into business for myself. I wanted

the money to go for myself. I sold heroin and coke. I also got back into prostitution. I had a house that became my father's rival. Because of the house, the girls only had to give me like $200. They made between $600 or $700 a night. You know what I'm sayin'. I just wanted $200 and that was it, cause I know how the hustle goes. I was clearing $4500 to $5500 a week.

I was still running my business, my old business, but it wasn't lucrative enough; cause people ... it was like crack then. So I got turned on to it. I had to look at it like, well, how can I like turn this into money, not only get high, but to maintain my style. I met this man, this old man, and he taught me how to cook up coke, how to bottle it, and how to sell it. For the first month, I only made like, just about $1000. Just enough to re-up and to buy me an outfit. And that wasn't good enough for me. Before I knew it, I was sellin'. I was makin' $6500 per week, if not better. Then I got workers.

I had workers in the street and at night I had another house that they'd work out of, uh, as long as I paid the girl's rent, which is only $250. Nobody sold out of my house. I couldn't have police comin' here. I had ten people that worked for me. I had five, let me get it right, I had four runners. Four muscles, very strong and very capable people. And two people that sat in the house with me. The muscle was generally the men. The others were girls I went to school with, girls I trusted, girls I did shit with.

For other women, drug use exerted a strong influence on their ultimate commitment to the illegal economy over employment in the secondary labor market. Even at the outset, commitment to licit work was weak. But, with the onset of cocaine smoking, such investments diminished and quickly disappeared. Barbara's involvement in legitimate work ended with her abuse of crack:

I worked for the Board of Education as a teacher's aide from like '84 to '86. When I was working I didn't need to be involved in crime at that time because I had my own income. But I was smoking crack. I was fired from the Board of Ed because of my lateness and absenteeism. I went back on Welfare.

I got so involved in getting high that I was kind of glad that I didn't have to get up in the morning anymore. I didn't care about that job or those people on that job, or even the kids like I was supposed to. I didn't care about a lot of things, and I preferred layin' home and waitin' for a check to come even as it was much less than what I was gettin' from the Board of Ed. It was like $400 compared to $150. That's when I started gettin' into dealing.

I never went back to working legal once things ended with the Board of Ed. I was only interested in how to make a living through hustles and scams. And, I was only interested in getting the money for the crack.

As we have heard, cocaine smoking intensified the illicit activities in which they already were active. Evelyn recalls:

> What happen was I didn't have any money, I didn't have any way of getting a job, I was already addicted into crack. Like I said, my parents threw me out of the house, there was no way means of getting any money from them or anything like that, I had bumped into people who were selling, and I got connected with them Two Spots selling drugs with their bosses. I said can help you out, be your look out or whatever, and from there I started working and I met the bosses and I started working like that.
>
> I would look out for them and I say listen I will look out for your back if you give me so and so. They didn't't want you smoking when you were selling, they wanted you to get rid of their stuff, and then you could smoke after you finished selling their stuff if not you would get physically hurt.

While the women's stories show that illicit behaviors were continuous over time, their intensification suggests some important transitions. These transitions were structured by economic changes and social opportunities as well as key developments within drug markets. The development of the cocaine economy created opportunities for drug selling that did not exist in prior, especially heroin, markets. The changing economic structure of inner city neighborhoods also created the possibility of changes in gender roles that in the past determined options for status and income within street drug networks.

At one time, women were excluded from selling by rigid gender roles and male hegemony in deviant street networks. The expanding cocaine economy and the increasing presence of women in the public domain may have neutralized the social processes that in the past consigned them to secondary roles in street networks. As a result, the women were able to form new organizations for drug selling, or pursue independent careers in drug selling.

For Gayle, making money through drug selling was her career ambition:

> I sold all kinds of drugs. I knew from the start that wanted to be big in this. From weed I went to selling heroin and to coke. I started dealing weed at 15. I used to steal weed from my father and deal it. Somebody approached me to deal crank (speed). I was making $200 a week. This guy provided the speed. I sold in this parking lot where kids hung out. I made $800 to $900 a week from speed.
>
> Then I sold heroin. I already had the knowledge of dealing. I went straight to somebody who sold heroin. The idea was strictly to make money.

I knew a guy who sold heroin. At first I sold it myself. Then I would cut ounces and bag it and let my female friends sell it for me off the street. I was making $2500 a week. I dealt heroin for years and I started dealing coke. At this point I really learned how to make lots of money selling drugs.

Viewing women's involvement in drug markets in economic and career terms suggests an active role in decision-making. Earlier deterministic conceptions of women and drugs described a passive drift into the secondary roles of hustling and prostitution in a street world dominated by men. However, the accounts provided by the women, indicate that within contemporary drug markets, women made decisions to enter based on a logical evaluation of career options. Here, the women considered both economic (wages) and non-pecuniary (status) returns from work in the secondary labor market. Furthermore, they realistically assessed their chances of obtaining economic and social support from domestic arrangements. Recognizing their constrained options, these women opted for illicit work which to them seemed to represent a rational choice.

Stephanie's account reflects this weighing of options:

Well I've been working off and on in different cashiers and stuff like since I'm 15 years old. I always knew that a woman couldn't depend on a man to take care of her. I grew up on Public Assistance. I saw how it affected my mom when we on PA. People always coming to check up on your home. And then I remember going all the way down somewhere, someplace she had to go to be interviewed for something, but I remember her sitting in front of these people and she began to cry. And, and I just couldn't understand why they were putting her through all this. And I know it was about money. It was about money for her children. And that hurt me, I never liked going through that. I hated having to go to the 'face-to-face.' I hated even the phrase.

So, I knew I would have to get a career or something. But work was just menial jobs to me, and they really didn't matter. I never liked, really liked clerical work and the sittin' down jobs. I left after about two years and did hair. But that was not getting me anything.

Shoplifting was a real big, a big high for me. Even after a day of work and making good tips, I still shoplifted. Occasionally I forged a few checks. But shoplifting basically was like, that was just, that became in the blood after a while. I really got high off of getting over in stores and things; and many times I had plenty money in my pocket, and I would still go and steal things. People noticed how fine I was looking. People also noticed my talent for taking stuff. I was getting a reputation, respect, on the street.

But then I saw that dealing drugs was a way to make real money. I wasn't goin' to be on PA. I started freelancing. I purchased coke from a guy that I used to cop for myself. He had a lot of influential people used to come and cop drugs from him. So I began to bring people to him. So at first I was like a steerer. But since I still had a job, in the hair business there's a lot of drugs flowing. So I used to just buy in large quantities and sell to people at work. I sold to people I knew, who I knew were into drugs. They would get it from me right then and there. And this went on during the course of the day. When I got off from work, I usually went to a friend's house that I know got high. I sat and got high with them, and I usually sold to whoever was in their home.

For Stephanie and many of the other women, criminal career choices provided them with higher incomes than were reachable by their peers in conventional careers. Furthermore, their involvement and success in these career trajectories placed them in contexts offering status (Hanson 1985; Williams 1989; Padilla 1992) excitement (Adler 1985; Anderson 1990), and commodities.

Dealing also helped many women avoid or exit from the types of street hustling, including prostitution, that characterized women's illicit income generating strategies. It freed some of the women from oppressive domestic partnerships and provided new ways for women to expand their traditionally limited roles, statuses and incomes in the street economy.

For many of the women in our study, however, their involvement in the workaday world of criminal enterprise was shortlived. The same drug--crack--that opened new career opportunities for a lot of them, also brought many of them down. Crack use resulted in their immersion in a social world where options became narrower and exploitation more likely (Rosenbaum 1981). The narrowing options reflected both the social contexts where crack was used and the effects of the drug itself.

Similar to heroin use in past eras, heavy crack use closed off social exits from drug use or hustling. One woman said that the intense pleasure from smoking crack, and the reinforcement when it was repeated, made it impossible "to make any space between [herself] and the world where [she] smoked it."

Reinarman et al. (1989) described the isolation that accompanies obsessive crack use, the suspicions toward friends and family members, the withdrawal from social interactions, the rejection of activities that do not lead to refilling the pipe, and the cashing in of limited economic and social assets in pursuit of an elusive but mythically powerful high. Thus, it is not surprising that with an increase in crack use, prostitution returned as an important income source for the women who used crack.

Prolonged crack use eventually led to deeper immersion in the social scenes and behaviors that limited their participation in both the licit and illicit work and social worlds. Although some walked away from crack after experimentation or maintained limits on their use of crack, others immersed themselves in crack use and reconstructed their social and economic lives to accommodate their frequent crack use.

The point of immersion into crack into the world of crack was an important turning point for the women in our study. Their *economic* lives, for instance, became increasingly intertwined with their *social* worlds. They organized their lives around drugs and immersed themselves in those activities and with those people with whom they shared economic and social behaviors. Their roles and identities, as well as their primary sources of status and income, became defined, exclusively, within these street networks. Their options for transition to legal work, marriage, or educational settings were limited. And, their engulfment in street networks reinforced their pathway into an abyss. Any notion of a "calculus" disappeared as "chasing the pipe" became the one and only goal of daily life.

For the majority of women, then, the problem of maintaining an addiction came to take precedence over other interests and participation in both the legal and illegal work worlds. The women also came to define themselves in relationship to their drug problems. They were "junkies," "crackheads," or "cokebitches." Few women, came to see themselves as criminals, workers, or in any way other than as addicts. Whatever deviant behaviors they engaged in came to be justified by their "drug compulsion."

The increased salience or primacy of their drug habits led to their "role engulfment". Schur has pointed out that one major consequence of the processes through which deviant identity is ascribed is the tendency "of the deviator to become 'caught up in' a deviant role ... that his behavior is increasingly organized 'around' the role ... and that cultural expectations attached to the role come to have precedence in the organization of his general way of life" (Schur, 1971:69). As a result, the women progressively became totally immersed in the networks of the drug markets. They became committed to the drug world's norms, values, and lifestyle, and they limited their involvement with nondeviant individuals and groups.

As the circumstances of the women's lives changed, and they became more engulfed in the drug world, it became less and less likely that they actively considered working, even at crime. Thus, for the majority of the women in our study, the short period between adolescence and adulthood took them through various positions vis-a-vis the workaday worlds. For many there was, indeed, any early engagement in the legal economy; all went on to embrace the social and pecuniary benefits of criminal participation; and most disengaged totally from both economies, immersed instead in an all consuming search for the next hit of crack.

As members of distinct communities where there are high levels of family dysfunction, economic dislocation and crime as well as where violence is frequently an organizing factor, these women devised ways of negotiating the demands of everyday life. In light of recent transformations in structural and situationally determined social norms, especially as they relate to gender, women in these particular communities, found space for themselves within the omnipresent drug markets.

Chapter 6

LIVING THE LIFE

Everybody engages in activities that organize their daily lives. For many of us, these activities center on making a living and/or being in school, creating and sustaining family life, seeking spirituality, performing civic responsibilities, and engaging in recreational activities. Most of us try to keep these activities in some sort of balance; although work and family life seem to occupy the majority of our days. Furthermore, most of us, on a daily basis, pay some attention to our own well-being and self-presentation. We eat, take care of personal hygiene, make sure we're adequately clothed and seek medical attention when we deem it necessary.

As we have seen in the preceding chapters, the women with whom we spoke, often grew up in settings where these activities, although perhaps cherished or valued, did not define their daily lives. For instance, the overwhelming majority of the women grew up in families where neither parents nor siblings routinely worked or attended vocational or educational programs. Furthermore, family life was characteristically distressed. There was an inordinate amount of physical and sexual abuse, drug, alcohol, and mental health problems, and often, parental or sibling criminality. Few of the women report having grown up attending church regularly and none of them recalled parental interest in civic associations, such as political clubs, school organizations, such as parent-teacher associations, or volunteer opportunities.

Many of the women reported taking care of their own daily needs at an early age, and some even took over responsibility for the care of younger siblings. Medical attention was sporadic and typically obtained in a hospital emergency room setting. None of the women reported having a family physician or pediatrician whom they saw on a routine basis. Dental care and orthodontics were unheard of, except for the former, when teeth required extraction. As gloomy as all of this sounds, their lives worsened as they left their families of origin and legitimate work environments and became more deeply entrenched in street life.

In this chapter, we turn to the descriptions that the women gave of their daily lives as adults. As you know already, by the time these women reached their mid-twenties, their attachments to the mainstream workaday world and/or conjugal arrangements were already attenuated if not completely severed. For 94%, drug addiction had firmly taken hold of their lives; for those who had children (81%), all had either lost or given up custody of them; for those who had been married or living as married (17%), these relationships were over. Friends were replaced by "associates" and contact with prosocial individuals and even their street families of origin became minimal at best, nonexistent in general.

Over the course of their twenties, the women reported a waning interest in clothes, jewelry and the high life. Their physical and mental health deteriorated. Many reported tremendous and rapid weight loss, bouts of pneumonia, HIV infection, and mental hospitalizations. For 84% of the women, during their twenties they experienced the bulk of their incarcerations (the median number of incarcerations was three and the median total time incarcerated was 19.7 months). And, during the course of these interviews, they regularly lamented that they were "tired."

ESTRANGEMENT FROM FAMILY LIFE AND PROSOCIAL RELATIONS

By the time these women were in their twenties, they were emotionally if not physically estranged from their foster or families of origin. Separation did not occur in the same manner as for most of us. These women did not go off to live in college dormitories nor did they leave to set up conjugal households. They did not answer advertisements for roommates that appeared in their community newspapers or in the Village Voice, nor did they set up apartments with friends from work or the neighborhood.

By and large, their estrangement followed several patterns: the women would maintain legal residence with their families but live most of the time on the street or in and out of the apartments of friends, lovers or other strangers; or these women would be kicked out of their families' households due to their involvement in drugs and/or crime, most often leaving their children behind; or they drifted in the streets, living in abandoned buildings, welfare hotels or, shelters. This movement in and out of shelters and the streets was often the end of the process in which these women became estranged from their families and prosocial friends.

There were a few women, with children, who left their "always nagging and interfering" families when welfare found them and their children an apartment in the projects. And, for those fortunate and very few who were lucky enough to have a steady income from drug dealing, they moved into public housing or low income apartments. However, for the majority of these women, their continued involvement in drug dealing and subsequent arrests and evictions often pushed them into the streets.

One thing was clear though, when speaking about families, parents, children, lovers, these people were viewed as fetters--fetters on these women's engagement, initially in the high life, and later on, in their missions to obtain drugs and stay high. Further, as these women became increasingly immersed in street life, their "associates" were people who also lacked the economic and social resources to help out during rough times.

Darlene's estrangement from her family was typical. She and her children drifted in and out of her mother's apartment in the projects to the apartments of various lovers. Eventually, in order to chase her high, she left her children and moved to the street. During the 7 years she was on the street, Darlene moved in and out of jail, detox, and mental hospitals, always returning to the street and becoming more deeply engulfed in street life. By the time of the interview, she no longer had contact with her mother or children. She occasionally saw one of her sisters and a niece, both of whom had serious addiction problems. She reported visiting with them only for the purpose of getting high. Further, she expressed her lack of interest in establishing prosocial relationships, getting married, or being reunited with her children. Her only interest was in getting and staying high.

> I have four kids--three boys and one girl. One will be 11, the next one 10, the next one will be nine, and my baby will be 7. They all live with my

mother. Um, I turned them over to her when I started smokin' crack. Until then, I lived with my mother or with the kids' fathers. They have 3 different fathers. Uh, the first two father, Pablo, I was with since I was like...we grew up. He was into smokin' angel dust. We would fight. I had a fractured jaw, broken ribs and I just chose to move back with my mother when I got pregnant again. The third one's father--we would just get high together. We would smoke Lace, uh, marijuana and cocaine. And, he was more or less a playboy. Then I met my daughter's father. Didn't see him for long.

I used to leave these kids all the time with my mother, you know. I just wanted to get high and they got in the way. I just left them and never came back. Then, I went to the street. Really got into robberies then, boostin' heavy, you know. Then I went to Rikers for robbery. Stayed for 67 days. I came back on the street still smokin' crack.

When I am livin' on the street, I usually sleep on abandoned lots, buildings. I eat out of dumpsters if there is nothing else. If I am living in a lot, I can sleep in the cars or steal parts from the cars and sell them.

Uh, I went to detox a couple of times but I was quickly back on the street smokin' crack. Was robbin' all the time. I was in the bullpen on and off and then I got sent away again, this time for a year--for a burglary. I came up and in no time, I ended up in the psychiatric unit in Coney Island Hospital. They locked me to my bed.

Then, I was living with, uh, this guy, his children's mother and his kids. It got to the point when he was out so that none of us could have him. I went back to the street and was on a run. I was chasin' the dragon, robbin', boostin', selling crack, and that is where I am today. I have no time for anythin' else. The only men I'm with now are the ones who can get me high-- I don't even care about the money. Sometimes I live with them for as long as they'll get me high. I sell myself for the drugs. Came here, today, because the money's good. The bottom line is that you do what you need to do to get the drugs. If one thing doesn't work out, you do the next best thing.

Doing the next best thing often meant stealing from those around you. Family members were seen as easy prey--that is, until they realized that they were being stolen from. Alicia, like many of the women who maintained legal residence with their parent(s) reported stealing from her mother in order to supplement her crime income to buy drugs:

Well, when I was in my early 20s, I was still really livin' with my mother, although I was out of there more than I was there and I started stealin' from her to buy drugs. She's a drunk and I started stealin' from her. Then she had a stroke so, for awhile, I had to take care of her. I was hangin' out at home, lookin' at soap operas, my friends would come over, we'd take my mother's welfare money and we'd get high, drink some beers. Then, my mother threw me out when she figured out what was happenin' to her money.

Haven't seen her since. And, my brothers and sisters, they're too straight to bother with. And, anyway, they got used to my being gone, you know.

Once thrown out by her mother, Alicia severed ties to her family and committed herself to running and living on the streets. While in the streets and much like Darlene, Alicia's life was punctuated by institutional experiences. However, Alicia, like most of the women in our study, refused to notify family members when she was in trouble, hospitalized or incarcerated.

When I went to the streets, I really took to robbin' people. Not just other kids like I did when I was in school. Went to Riker's 13 times. Usually had stays of 6 months at a time. I was in Kings County [mental hospital] twice 'cause I felt like killin' someone. And, another couple of times because they said I had manic-depression. But I was just tired. Usually when I got out, I would be sent to a shelter. It was the pits. But I ain't never want to go back home. My family would never come see me and I never used to call them. I didn't even tell them where I was, you know.

Alicia, like the other women who were estranged from their families, often moved. Some moved from shelter to shelter, SRO to SRO, lover to lover, or couch to couch in the apartments of various "associates". Others lived "nowhere", crashing each day wherever their last drug hit took place. A few ended up in crackhouses or alone, on the street. Alicia describes her path to the crackhouse.

Then I met this guy. Lived with him for 5 years. Then I was into hustlin'. I was seein' other people, you know. But I didn't care what he thought. There was no feeling. Then, I moved into the crackhouse. People tell me there, "you know, you're not a bad lookin' girl. You know, why don't you get yourself together." Sometimes I thought they cared. But they're in the life just like me. Really, I don't know anybody who isn't in the life. Just got out of Woodhull [mental hospital] but it made no difference. I'm back at a different crackhouse because we got evicted from the other one.

L.G. left her mother's apartment in the housing project when welfare provided her with funding to set up a household with her children in a hotel.

I have a 6 year old daughter and a son is eleven. They're under kinship foster care with my mother. They used to live with me in a welfare hotel. It took me a while to get this apartment for me and my kids. I wanted to be out from under my mother--she was always talkin' about my runnin' around. So, to use my benefits, I figured moving to a welfare hotel would be a step towards gettin' out.

I moved into the welfare hotel and got involved with the wrong people. They was loansharkin' and really druggin'. I borrowed money from them but I didn't want to pay them back. All I wanted was to get high.

Welfare hotels are notorious for their criminogenic properties. Further, they have been shown to initiate, support and even amplify resident involvement in other forms of deviant behavior, including drug abuse. For instance, Zimmer and Schretzman (1991:174) characterized them as having an "abnormal ambience" that constantly "assaults" the residents with exposure to and pressure from drug dealers, loansharks, and pimps. The tension of living in these environments often increased the use of drugs "which in turn creates a spiral of seemingly insurmountable problems (Zimmer and Schretzman, 1991:174). Children and their needs were increasingly viewed by the women in our study as one set of such problems.

This was certainly the case for L.G.:

> Lots of times, I would go off and get high and not come back for my kids. One time the courts took my kids away for that. The hotel people had called the cops because they thought something had happened to me when I didn't come back for my kids. The kids have two different fathers who are with other women. One is married.
>
> You know, I can't see my kids anymore. They say I'm an abusive mother because I neglected them. I like my children, really. But I like crack more. They were just gettin' in the way.

Accounts of children getting in the way abounded. As Stephanie told us:

> I have two kids, one 11, one 5. Two girls. They live with my mother because I became really strung out really bad on drugs. They went to live with my mother when the 5 year old was born. They have no relations with their fathers. The first one had a wife and other children. Because I didn't have time for her 'cause I was always running, at first, the 11 year old would sometimes go and stay with her father and his wife and their kids. But her father began his drug abuse and he really got out of hand and left. He just disappeared. The second kid, her father, he recently died of AIDS.

Wanda, too, told us of her son:

> Yeah, I have a son. I have been away from him for 5 years while I've been runnin' the streets, druggin' and doin' things like that. I was never with my son. He lives with his grandmother. BCW took him away from me. My mother called them because I was neglectin' him. I was abandonin' him to go get high.

Sharon shared with us the following account:

> I have 2 children, 2 and 8. They're in foster care. The 2 year old has always been with foster parents. The 8 year old lived with me for awhile. I was selling drugs and I was more involved with what was happening with me on the streets. I was living in a house I was selling and doing other things from. So, I left her with my sister and paid my sister for taking care of my daughter. But then my sister moved to Philadelphia and I tried to pass custody over to her so she could get more benefits from public assistance. So her father appeared in court and I didn't. They took custody from my sister. But the father never came to get her from my sister. And then I took her back. I was getting higher and higher and not coming back to the house so the courts took her back again. So foster care has the children. The youngest one don't know who her father is. When I was pregnant with her, I would feel her moving in my stomach and I would get high even more just to knock her out.

It was clear from the accounts provided by the women, especially those who were addicted to crack, that they were not going to allow anyone or any condition to stand in their way of getting high. Further, they were willing to do absolutely anything in order to obtain drugs. Barbara describes how her relationship with her father changed when she became a crackhead:

> When crack came out people were willing to do anything for it. Women were so willing to sell their bodies for this drug. Old men just flipped. They just got they shit off--my father was one of them. And, he started looking at me more like a crackhead than like a daughter. And, one day, I was, uh, I was out there. I was on a mission as they call it. And, I went to him and I needed some money. And he wasn't willing to give me money like he used to. And he told me that I would have to have sex with him if I wanted some money from him. And, I did. He moved in with me for awhile and we traded sex for drug money. Then he got disgusted with me and I haven't seen him since. Haven't seen any of my family since.

Accounts such as this one were not unusual. As these women became increasingly addicted to crack, their interactions with family members and or formerly close friends became ancillary to their crack quest. Relations with family and friends, as well as their motivations for sex, their choice of housing arrangements and income generation activities all became organized around their desires to get high. Over and over they traded sex, apartments, anything else they could to get high. They began relationships and they ended them all in terms of how they fit into their drug world. They moved in and out of criminal activities based on their drug needs. Many re(turned) to prostitution, often for the human contact it provided. As April recounted:

> I turned to prostitution from dealing because it was easy, and uh, it kind of like, uh, it gave me company. That was something I didn't get from dealing. I would always be with somebody that used the drug theirself but who had money to support their habit. I would sleep with anyone who had drugs or the money to buy them.

In terms of their relations with their children, the women reported having had serial abortions, neglecting their children, and often abandoning them, again and again, because they, the children, affected their ability to get and stay high. Although a few women reported abstaining temporarily or at least minimizing their drug intake during pregnancy, many viewed the growing fetus with disdain, already anticipating a future of neglect and abandonment. As Monica told us:

> With my last child, I got high even more behind her. I would feel her moving in my stomach and I would get high even more just to see what she would do. Sometimes I would get even higher just like to knock her out, you know. But, really, I just kept getting high while I was pregnant 'cause I wanted to. I liked it.

This type of an account, where pregnant crack addicts reported taking advantage of their pregnancies to obtain free hits of crack and food or sexually entice customers to the sex trade has been noted by other researchers (Bourgois and Dunlap,1993).

In general, most of the study women who were addicted to crack had no one upon whom they could rely. They had short-lived associations, some with people who abused and tried to control them through access to drugs and with people, who like themselves, would do anything to get high. Some of them moved into crackhouses where they would exchange sex for food, shelter and drugs. These accommodations, too, were often temporary. Often the women fought with the crackhouse owner or manager leading to their being thrown out. Or, the owner/manager would lose his/her lease and all of the occupants would be evicted. Sometimes, police raids would close down crackhouses, throwing residents onto the streets.

Over and over, the women in our study reported being victimized precisely by the people with whom they were associating--people who they initially, they sought out to replace "family" and meet their instrumental and expressive needs. By the time we had interviewed these women, ties to family and friends had been broken and all relationships or "associations" had become commodified and were viewed with suspicion.

THE ORGANIZATION OF DAILY LIFE

Broadly characterized, the women in our study organized their lives during adulthood in two different ways. There were those women for whom the *mission* to obtain drugs and stay high was all consuming. For these women, the manner in which they secured drugs, usually crack, was unimportant. Each day began with the quest to obtain drugs by any and all means. And, each day might have required different means. If all else failed, these women were ready to resort to prostitution in order to get their high.

The other group of women settled into drug dealing as an outgrowth of their prior involvement in street crime. Their long term experience on the street, the ease with which they traversed the different worlds of street life, and their familiarity and willingness to use weapons, both to protect themselves and their "interests" made them attractive to established drug dealers who were looking to expand their crews or finance off shoots. Therefore, it was in the context of dealing that the women from this group supported and kept control over their drug habits.

Women on a mission: Drugs first, all else, unimportant

The majority of the women in our study had a history of polydrug use. By the time of the interview, 72% of all of the women reported being addicted to crack, 49% to powdered cocaine, and 40% to heroin. However, there were notable differences in the timing and processes associated with their addictions. Among women who entered the street scene later in their lives, addiction took hold during their very late teens or early 20s and centered almost exclusively on crack. For these women, entrenchment in violent street crime was pushed by their drug involvement. And, for these women, estrangement from conventional activities occurred more rapidly and reached its peak sooner than for the early onset women.

The desperation to obtain crack among these women led them to burglarize and rob anybody and anything, using whatever force was necessary. Further, their crack addiction shattered whatever ties they had to prosocial activities and individuals faster and sooner than it did for the women who entered the street scene earlier. Women in the former group were more likely to steal from family members, abandon their children without a second thought, and end up alone, and on the street sooner than their earlier onset counterparts.

One cannot underestimate the impact that crack addiction had on its users. Unlike addiction to other drugs, crack produces an aggressively antisocial posture that has been characterized as greedy, obsessive, desperate, and immoral. Crack addicts, always chasing the rush they first experienced when they were initiated into crack smoking, are routinely suspicious of others, taking more than their share or of stealing from them. As a result, and as their addiction intensifies, they do anything they feel they need to in order to protect their drugs and or opportunities to get high. Eventually, they cut themselves off from all but the person who is, at that moment, supplying them. Long term crack addiction, left unchecked, leads its users further down the road of social isolation(Bourgois, 1995; Dunlap, 1992; Hamid, 1992; Ratner, 1993; Waldorf, et al., 1991). As Gazella recounted:

> It's different with this crack thing. I used heroin for so many years. When I started using crack, there are things that I did, that it's like, immoral. You know, it's like some strange sick shit and I did things that I never thought I would do in my life.

Thus, unlike addiction during earlier drug eras, the women in our study found themselves in the midst of one that has been characterized in all available research as the most desperate, demeaning and degrading of all drug contexts. The all-encompassing fixation on procuring crack placed these women in a street scene characterized by violence, victimization and hopelessness. This can be seen in the accounts of daily life given by these women. Darlene shared with us, her typical day:

> Madness, pure madness! And all my money went to my crack. I was smoking as much as I could get my hands on. Sometimes, $300, sometimes, $1000 a day.
>
> I've been livin' on the street most of the time. I've sleep in abandoned lots, buildings. I eat out of dumpsters. If I'm sleepin' in a lot, I steal parts from cars. I also take from stores. If you saw something in the store that you can get, you know, you get it. You know you gonna make some money for it. Doesn't matter how much, just as long as you make something.
>
> When I can, I set up burglaries. I try to set up people I know. It always works better that way. I always carry a blackjack. Sometimes I do them with somebody. And then we'd get high together. But usually, I don't hang around with a lot of people, so I usually do stuff alone. That way, I don't need to share my stuff.
>
> I'll give you an example. My next door neighbor, you know, I grew up. The lady's been living there all her life. I grew up going to the store for her and doing stuff for her. On this particular day, I went to her house. I went to the store for her and I took her keys and I left. And I knew where she kept her money and everything. And I waited for her to go to sleep. It was like no big thing. Another time, I did a niece's boyfriend.
>
> I also snatch a lot of pocketbooks. When you're livin' on the streets you do what you can do. I wait for people who are coming from check cashing. You see, these people are easy prey, you know.
>
> When I'm dealing crack, you wake up, you know. You be behind a- steel door, workin' from under the door. Me, I would smoke some crack first, you know. I seen about a good thousand people a day, you know. Maybe the same people over and over, but a thousand people a day.
>
> There was lot of violence in it, everyday. In the building I worked they were selling. I see young ladies getting beat down a with a gun--the butt of a gun for going over her limit, you know. I seen shoot outs. I seen the guys that I work for ride up on somebody and shoot them for owin' them money or, you know, tryin' to set them up--that type of stuff. Again, when you live in that, like, kind of neighborhood where I was running the streets in, you see a lot of that. You figure like this--it's not you, and you leave it alone, okay.
>
> I also do some street corner prostitution. I sell my body a lot. I do all this for crack. Sometimes, I didn't even want the money--just the crack.
>
> On days that don't go right and I need more money, I do more prostitution. You do the next best thing to get that money. Sometimes, I stash things for people. Anything. That's part of the whole thing. Everyday is something like this. Always doing something to get high.

Darlene, like many of the women in our study, was primarily preoccupied with getting high. She reported her willingness to use any and all means that might provide her with drugs. Although she was involved in drug dealing, it really was tangential to her primary quest for crack. This was true, also, for Wanda:

> I wake up and immediately I have to have me a hit of crack. Everyday. And, once I get that, my day starts right there. I be like as they say, on a mission. I be wantin' more and more and more, you know. I hang out all day and all night lookin' for opportunities to get more or to get high. Everyday I shoplift. If I am high, I be stealin' and robbin' all day long. Or, I be on a street corner, wave my hand and sell myself.

Gazella described her typical day similarly:

> I woke up in the morning, uh, I went a couple of blocks from my house. I picked up my drugs and I'd get off. That was most important--doing my drugs first. Then I'd start selling, I had like a shift. When work was done, I'd get high again. Then I'd go to sleep--on the street--I hardly ever went home. Sometimes, I would go take stuff from a store or meet some people to do a burglary. I was always high. Sometimes, we'd even take out weapons and just go out robbin' people. And, if I got angry at someone, or they disrespected me, I beat them. Then, I wasn't high. My days were just one thing after another. Sometimes, I'd be sellin' my body, sometimes I'd be holdin' stolen stuff for people, I even set a fire for money. Some of this stuff was for excitement too. But, the most important thing was for getting high.

The expense of crack addiction is enormous. Among the women we studied, they reported that over the three year period of time preceding the interview, they used, on the average, almost $3000 worth of crack a week. Spending hundreds of dollars in a few hours, fencing stolen goods for a few cents of what they were worth, stealing from anybody and anything, tell us something about the desperation that organized their daily life.

Drug Dealing First

For most of the women, involvement in drug dealing emerged out of their more generalized participation in street crime. As these women got older, they moved from being involved in street crimes such as shoplifting and robbery for excitement and adventure, to participation as a way of making a living.

This, too, can be said of their involvement in drug dealing. Dealing expanded their repertoire of activities that, for many, at least initially, provided income for living expenses and then, later, for most, to support their burgeoning drug habits.

Denise made it big in the drug distribution market. Here, she described her typical day:

> I get up a seven. I work out, have breakfast, shower, decide what I'm gonna wear--call all around to see who got what. Everybody's meetin' at my house to count out money and we have a little coffee, a little small brunch, count out money and see where everybody's at. Then I make a run. But before that I go down to my closet where I keep the files on who's short and how often. Then, on my way out, I stop and give the kids in the neighborhood $10. I sit up on my little fuckin' Benz and I talk shit to the niggers and play the radio and maybe go for a ride.
>
> If it is a day when someone has been short 4 or 5 times, then I have to take care of them. If they smokin' my stuff, I take care of them. I whup they fuckin' ass and I'm cuttin' they shit up. Same goes for rival dealers--I 'd go shoot your shit up. I'd go tear your place up. I'd stick up your workers. I'd cut up they clothes. I'd take your shit and I'd do it everyday until you either moved or you came to work for me.
>
> I like nines. I like barringers with nickel plated handles. I like style and something that works well. A woman can catch a bad one if she ain't prepared. I have rules--don't steal from me--ask me for something and I'll given it to you but don't steal from me. I have this one West Indian girl and I pay her $750 plus anything she want to eat. If she saw an outfit she wanted, she got it. She never skimmed from me and she never took from me neither. When all's done, I settle in and smoke-- about $1000/day. That's a typical day, on a rampage, I smoke more.

Denise ran her own drug dealing organization. Her day was typical of the women crew bosses. Of the women in our study, 44% had, at one time or another, managed their own dealing organization. Often, the women who were in management roles or who routinely committed part of their days to drug dealing refrained from getting too high during their shifts for fear of being vulnerable or not being able to take full advantage of situations. Even among those who initially organized their days around getting high, opportunities to climb in drug organizations, often acted to suppress their use.

Monica used to organize her day around getting high. Eventually, though, she seized an opportunity to start her own drug business and got high only when business was taken care of:

Okay, at first, I'd get up and get high 'cause that would be the first thing I'd always do. Get high on crack. I also smoked lots of Willows--which is reefer inside a cigar. So, I'd get up, smoke, get dressed and just go out, pick up drugs and start working. When I wasn't dealing, I was basically just getting high and not doing anything. Then, after a while, I started my own business. From dealin' on the street, I got to know people and they trusted me. I had to keep my gettin' high under control so that I could run this business. But once the day, was done, I was getting high.

Angie described her day similarly:

Well I get up 7 o'clock in the morning. And being that I had a drug habit, I had a make myself straight, so by 7:30 the bosses were coming upstairs cuz the drugs and everything were in my apartment, so they would come upstairs and he would ask who I wanted to work with, you know, who's gonna be the lookouts, who's gonna be the gunman, the runner stuff like that, so I would give them certain names, who I wanted to work with, and we had a big safe with drugs and money and everything, and he would go into the safe and he would give me my drugs I needed to make myself straight. And he would count out what I'm going to take to sell, and what money was in there and everything, and he would you know, write down everything all the workers names and how much they were going to get paid for the day. By 8 or 8:30 we would go downstairs and we had a spot in the building, I mean people lived there, but we had the whole second floor it was an empty apartment. I use to go in there to sell the drugs. And then we had two look-out mans, we had one on each floor, looking out for the cops, and when I come out of my building, to go into the other building to go deal drugs, I mean everybody would be ready for me outside. Cuz are sick, they wanted to shoot heroin, whatever. Then I go into the building, then we you know everybody take their spot, wherever it is. Then we started selling drugs, bring in like five people at a time. You know this goes on until 8 o'clock that night. During the day you got argue here and there, but you got people coming back, saying that they were missing a bag and things like that or they gave me more money then they should of and then you got the look out man, the boss wanna know where he's at because um, he wasn't there ten minutes ago, he was suppose to be there. You know, It's like that. It goes all around and around in a circle and I gotta go back when that finishes. Bring the money there, and then count out more drugs, and that was the whole day.

That was it for the day, everybody got paid. Whoever wanted, um, they would tell my boss well you know, send three bags with her, or send five bags, everybody you know, tell them what they want and when we go up stairs, he's got the list, bring so and so two bags this or two bags of that. So I said I want five, here's pay, everybody's pay with whatever they want. Then everybody go home, wherever they were going, either home or they go out and hang out in the street, or go upstairs.

I would just go straight upstairs. You know, everything, all this action was going on right here in my house, with the money and the drugs. So once my boss would leave and I would stay upstairs and go to the store and buy my food and eat, take a shower and, and you know, start the next day would be the same routine.

I really didn't have time like that in the morning I would get high, and then I say about, they use to give us a break in between, around 11 or 12 o'clock, whatever, or 10 or 11 o'clock it depends on how fast the drugs were sold. Then that time I would go upstairs and get more drugs, and put away the money, and I would put away the money, and I would get high and come back down, then at 1 o'clock or 2 o'clock I would come back down, so it was like 4 or 5 times a day I was getting high. So it was coming out to a lot of money, just getting high alone.

However, Janelle had a long history of involvement in street crime. And, she knew the importance of maintaining control if she was to be successful at both her "job" and at not getting victimized.

The typical day was like, you know, intense, 'cause you know you always have to watch your back. You have to make sure that people wasn't gonna rob you, wasn't goin' to stick you up. You couldn't be high and do the dealin' right. Especially if you're tryin' to get over on everyone--on the person you' workin' for, on the person you're dealin' to.

Unfortunately, not all of the women were able to maintain their upward mobility on the drug distribution ladder. As a result, many of them allowed their immersion in the world of drug dealing to lead them further into drug abuse. That was the case for Alicia:

I started livin' on the street when I got evicted. I started hangin' and meetin' people that's hustlin', dealin', prostitutin'. I first got into dealin' this way--just by hangin' on the street.

On a typical day, I'd wake up hang out all night and sleep all day till you go out at night. It was excitin'. The party, the ridin', doin' the after hour clubs, you know. Everybody start gettin' to know you.

There were a lot of shoot outs. A lot of violence when I was selling- especially when you sell crack. I had a five shot and a switchblade. Everybody's tryin' to get over . Everybody will stab you in the back you know. Nobody gives a fuck about the next person, you know. It's just when you want it, you want it. You know, when you want the drug, you know, you want the drug. There's a lot of lyin'. It's crazy. I'd use my weapon, sure. Especially when someone was tryin' to take my package.

When I first started dealin' I bought pretty clothes, did a lot of partyin'. But then, when I got into smokin' crack, all my profits went into smokin' and gettin' high. I was dealin' it right back. Once you start smokin' crack you don't care how you look. You only want that high.

Got to a point, when dealin' was takin' too much time away from gettin' high. So, I did it only on and off. Instead, I used to smoke on the streets, abandoned buildings, lots. Sometimes I'd pay people to go to they houses. I used to shoplift too to buy drugs. I used to go out everyday. I would burglarize too. I also stuck people up in their houses and on the street. You know, when they got paid, you know, maintenance workers, and social security checks. I always showed them a weapon, otherwise they wouldn't give you no damn money.

I had lots of uh, fights. I got hit with a bottle on my neck. I have the scars. I had a lot of fights, you know, especially when you are drinkin' and druggin'. I did lots of robberies when I was high, too. I wanted more drugs. I'd trade people the stuff for drugs. It's a lifestyle.

Well, what first I got into for excitement, I later stayed into because of drugs. And, I was addicted to crack. So, you sleep all day, or sometimes watch soap operas and talk. You just hang out waiting to get high again.

This pattern was recounted by many of the women. Getting high took priority over all else.

I was livin' on the street. I was hookin', shopliftin'. But I was really into robbin' people, you know. I also fought openly in the street. When I would be dealin' crack, I would go get my stuff and stand in the park holdin' bundles of crack. But first I had to do my own crack. The guy I would buy from would give me something first thin--sort of like a fix. I always needed to carry things to protect myself--knives, razors, clubs, little blackjacks.

While doing all this, I also got into stolen credit cards and stealin' from places of business when they were closed. also would do stick ups. For that, I needed to use a gun. I would do almost any crime to avoid a day of hookin'. I would rob you rather than perform a service. But if push came to shove I would do anything to get high. (Stephanie)

As getting high became all important, these women became even more preoccupied with "getting over" (Goldstein, 1985). By this time, many of them were completely estranged from friends and family. They had exhausted their access to the resources of associates. They were completely out of the loop as far as legitimate employment was concerned. And, some had difficulty in maintaining their support from public agencies, such as welfare. Their lives were hypermarked by conning, scheming, lying, predatory and non-predatory crime--both as victims and as offenders. They robbed, burglarized, dealt drugs, shoplifted, used stolen credits, forged checks, and when all else failed, or they were especially lonely and destitute, they engaged in prostitution.

During the course of their careers, the violence in the lives of these women increased. They themselves became more violent due to a synergy among the psychopharmacological, systemic and economic-compulsive effects of prolonged crack use, (Goldstein, 1985). These same effects and deeper entrenchment in the street world also resulted in their increased violent victimization.

THE CONSEQUENCES OF FAST LIVING

As we have seen, one of the unintended consequences, however, of dramatically increased access to drugs was the uncontrolled spiral of drug addiction. Most of the women with whom we spoke agreed that having constant cheap supplies on hand increased the danger that they would consume their profits and develop even more serious drug-related problems. Several people we interviewed did just that. L.G., Rhonda and Stephanie describe the predicament of using and selling crack.

> L.G.: I sold crack like for a percentage; uh, just to have some to smoke, I would sell. So that, you know, the person that I was selling for would allow me to have a certain amount for myself and then I had to sell a certain amount. So that just was like for my habit... There were times I got paid in cash. But if I made $200 cash, I smoked $180. So I never really got cash.
>
> Rhonda: I use to work with Diane and them, we use to sell nickel bottles, you know, then I would buy my own bundles, a bundle consists of 11 bottles. And if I want to I can either smoke it or sell it, most of the time I would smoke them! You know. I bought 3 bundles one time, that's $150.00, so I am like, I sole one bundle and smoked the rest.
>
> Stephanie: Like gettin' up in the morning, uh, looking for he guy you want to sell drugs for. By bein' a crackhead, of course, you're in need right now. You want to get high before you do anything. So he will give you the drugs. He will give you something to get you high. Then you will sell.
>
> You will sell ten and you will keep one. The faster you work, and the more efficient-- they don't like people too sloppy, like you're drawing large

crowds, and you're droppin' things, or you're too high, then you won't be able to do it. If you're workin real good, he doesn't mind to look out which means you'll eat god, you'll get clean clothes, you'll probably get a room to stay in at night, and you can get high. And that's basically all you're lookin' for when you're a crackhead.

The increase in drug availability (and use) gave rise to a lifestyle that was totally out of control.

> Janelle: When I first started dealin' I used to go shopping, buy clothes, buy jewelry, buy my brother and sister stuff. I wasn't doing anything but smokin' reefer. Smokin' crack changed everything. I would shoplift for clothes. Rob, burglarize, and deal. I used to carry a 38. I thought all of this was a joke. It all was part of more money and more reputation and more drugs.

> Wanda: I woke up and immediately I had to have me a hit of crack. Everyday. And, once I get that, my day starts right there. I be like as they say, on a mission. I be wantin' more and more and more, you know. I'd hang out all day and all night. We'd shoplift everyday. If I was high, I be stealin' all day long. Or, I'd be on a street corner, wave my hand and sell myself.

Although Jocorn had her own organization, increased drug use compelled her to look for additional income-generating hustles:

> I was running the organization. I had to find out from my people on the streets if anything was up, if they needed more drugs, or if they didn't have much money, or if it was too hot to deal. Once they were off and running for the day, I would do other things. I was a crook, I would steal cars, take from department stores, write out some bad checks or use some of the credit cards I would steal. Sometimes, I would get together with some people and we'd break into apartments. I was always down with the crime.

Nonetheless, drug selling was profitable. Drug incomes exceeded drug expenses. Again, however, drug selling clearly facilitated drug use, or may have provided an income source to meet the needs of heavy drug use. But the distinction may not be a meaningful one. The highly disciplined drug seller who avoided drug use seemed to be rare and elusive. Instead, a pattern of drug use combined with selling was more typical as a part of the social processes within these neighborhoods and among people who were involved in the local drug markets.

Despite its initial excitement and allure, street life was hard. A host of severe personal problems plagued most of the women. And, typically, it became progressively worse as their careers continued. Thus, the women's lives were dominated by a powerful, often incapacitating, need for drugs. Consequently, economic problems were the most frequent complaint voiced by the respondents. Savings were quickly exhausted and the culture of addiction justified the use of virtually any means to get money in order to support their habits.

For the majority of women, the problem of maintaining an addiction took precedence over all other interests and over participation in other social worlds. Their primary reference group, people they associated with, was involved in a wide range of illicit behaviors. Over time, the women became further enmeshed in deviance and further alienated, both socially and psychologically, from conventional life. The women's lives became bereft of conventional involvements, obligations, and responsibilities. The excitement of the lifestyle that may have characterized their early criminal career phase gave way to a much more serious and grave daily existence.

The following accounts illustrate the uncertainty and vulnerability of street life. Even for Denise, who ran her own drug organization, street life took its toll:

> I was in a lot of fights. So I had fights over, uh, drugs, or, you know, just manipulation. There's a lot of manipulation in that life. Everybody's tryin' to get over. Everybody will stab you in your back, you know. Nobody gives a fuck about the next person, you know. It's just when you want it, you want it. You know, when you want that drug, you know, you want that drug. There's a lot of lyin', a lot if manipulation. It's, it's, it's crazy! It also got frightening.

Gazella,

> I'm 34 years old. I ain't no young woman no more, man. Drugs have changed, lifestyles have changed. Kids are killing you now for turf. Yeah, turf, and I was destroyin' myself. I was miserable. I was . . . I was gettin' high all the time to stay up to keep the business going, and it was really nobody I could trust. Things kept getting worse and worse. Everything was spoiling around me.

Sonya provided an account of what daily life was like on the streets:

> You get tired of bein' tired, you know. I got tired of hustlin', you know. I got tired of livin' the way I was livin', you know. Due to your body, your body, mentally, emotionally, you know. Everybody's tryin' to get over. Everybody will stab you in your back. Nobody gives a fuck about the next person. And I used to have people talkin' to me, "you know, you're not a bad lookin' girl. You know, why you don't get yourself together."

Additional illustrations of the exigencies of street-life were provided by April and Stephanie.

> I wasn't eating. Sometimes I wouldn't eat for two or three days. And I would . . . a lot of times I wouldn't have the time, or I wouldn't want to spend the money to eat -- I've got to use it to get high. My teeth were falling out and I looked real bad. I never knew what was going to happen next--whether I would have something to eat, someplace to live, anything. (April)

Stephanie, had used and sold crack for five years:

> I knew that, uh, I was gonna get killed out here. I wasn't havin' no respect for myself. No one else was respecting me. Every relationship I got into, as long as I did drugs, it was gonna be constant disrespect involved, and it come . . . to the point of me gettin' killed. I had a few times when I thought that was going to happen--that was going to be the end of it.

The stereotypical image of the successful drug dealer is the "fast life." Clothes, jewelry, cars, houses, parties, are all part of this lavish lifestyle. However, few of the women we interviewed achieved this success; and even fewer were able to maintain it for any length of time even if success initially was achieved. Although many earned substantial sums of money from selling drugs, for most of the women, drug abuse and the exigencies of street life resulted in an overwhelming sense of personal despair and isolation.

Regardless of how the women were initiated into drug dealing, the vast majority ended up in the same role--as street addicts. The women became increasingly immersed in their addiction at the exclusion of almost all else. For instance, as their drug use expenses increased by 157%, the income they received from crime other than drug dealing declined, as did any remaining attempts at licit work. Here, they described their descent to rock bottom.

> My last year of living on the street, I went through massive changes. I began to sink. My self-esteem sank lower. I became pregnant in the street--as

a hooker. I had a baby at this hospital. The baby was born deformed. The baby died. I was havin' no respect for myself. No one else was respecting me. Every relationship I got into with a man, it was constant disrespect and it came to the point of almost gettin' me killed (Stephanie).

I was gettin' old--34. Drugs were changing. Lifestyles were changin'. Kids are killing you now for turf. A friend of mine was killed in a shoot out. I was destroying myself. I was miserable. I was gettin' high all the time to stay up to keep the business going and it was really nobody I could trust. And it was miserable. I was tired, I was run down, I was lookin bad. I smashed myself through a window and was sent to a psychiatric hospital. My hands were bandaged, my feet were bandaged. I had smashed myself through a 6th floor window (Denise).

I didn't have a place to live. I was so tired of living on the streets. My kids had been taken away forever. I was constantly being harassed by the police, like 3 days out of the week by TNT. I was so depressed. You know how you look bad and feel bad. Before, I had an apartment and other things. But now, nothing. I lost everything. I was at rock bottom. I was so tired of being tired.

Many of the women reported a noticeable deterioration in their physical health. As April recounted:

Oh, my appearance went down. I lost a lot of weight. I was about 100 pounds. I wasn't eating. Sometimes I wouldn't eat for two or three days. Alot of times, I wouldn't have the time, or I wouldn't want to spend the money to eat--I had to use it to get high.

Monica:

I was living in a homeless hotel. I was tired. I looked tired. I weighed like 92 points. Everyday I got up with like a hangover.

Others reported bouts with severe depression. They often thought they were losing their minds. As Alicia recalled:

So, I had gotten evicted again. I went to live in the park and I cried for 6 months. I didn't want to be bothered with people. I was always lyin', schemin' and stayin' in abandoned buildings in Bushwick. I got a bad depression 'cause I was sittin' around and lookin' at myself all day.

Darlene recalled being afraid of dying:

> I can tell you, I was afraid of dying. Here I was locked up in a psychiatric unit, locked to a bed. I was tired.

Marginalization from family, friends, children, and work-in short, the loss of traditional life structures- left many of the women vulnerable to chaotic street conditions. For a small few, the stresses of street life and the fear of dying on the streets motivated them to quit the criminal life.

Chapter 7

QUITTING THE LIFE

As we have seen in previous chapters, the trajectories of crime and drug behaviors for the women in our study reflected a shift in their social and economic relations. Their *economic* lives placed them increasingly in *social* worlds where they were distanced from legal work. Their everyday economic lives centered around the acquisition and consumption of drugs. They became immersed in street networks where their social interactions were increasingly limited to people involved in these economic and social behaviors. Their social roles and identities, as well as their primary sources of status and income, were increasingly defined within these street networks. In short, these women were locked into a deviant social world, having little stake in conventional life or conventional identity.

However, even the most persistent and lengthy criminal careers have a "natural" course, tapering off and eventually ceasing as they age, possibly "burning out" physically, and easing out of "the life." In this chapter, we offer a glimpse into the lives of 35 of the 156 study women who successfully exited the social world of crime and drugs.[8] We discuss a range of factors that

---

[8] A problematic aspect of the definition of desistance is its permanence. Termination that is followed by criminal involvement might be considered "false" (Blumstein et al., 1985). Elliott et al. (1989) have avoided the variable termination by using the variable suspension, a temporary or permanent cessation of criminal activity during a particular period of time. Clearly, we cannot know if the study women have demonstrated "true desistance." The data presented here does not warrant the conclusion that none of the women ever renewed their involvement in crime. That the study materials consisted of retrospective information with all its attendant problems, precludes stating with certainty whether desistance from crime is

affected their decisions to move out of deviance and their reintegration into mainstream society.

For these women, the decision to stop deviant behavior was preceded by a variety of factors. The majority of these factors revolved around social reactions to their behaviors. For instance, many of the women reported an increase in their formal contacts with the criminal justice system--from increased arrests, informal dispositions and even incarcerations. Other women reported increased difficulties in maintaining any sort of living arrangements, including the most basic shelter, food and clothing. Yet, for other women, the "final" threat of sanctions or complete withdrawal by family or close relations affected their decisions to desist. Most of the women also recalled a precipitous decline in their physical and mental health. A few stated that religious conversions or immersion into alternative socio-cultural settings with powerful norms (e.g., treatment ideology) provided paths for cessation.

There were several processes that sustained and reinforced the changed behaviors on the part of those who decided to quit. For some, simple changes in physical location and social networks precipitated desistance. For others, transformations of identity and the formation of ties to conventional lifestyles aided them in easing out of the life. Yet, several of the women reported that changes in the functional definitions of the problem behavior and displacement of the old behavior with new forms of behavior or expression (from religion, to physical outlets, to strong belief systems) were responsible for the transition. In this chapter we explore some of these factors with this subsample of women.

Resolving to Stop

Despite its initial excitement and allure, street life is hard. A host of severe personal problems plague most street offenders, and normally become progressively worse as their careers continue. In our study, the women's lives were dominated by a powerful, often incapacitating, need for drugs. Consequently, economic problems were the most frequent complaint voiced

---

permanent. Still, it also is clear that these women broke their pattern of involvement in crime for substantial lengths of time and have changed their lives. A two year hiatus from crime certainly indicates temporary cessation and more importantly it is a long enough period of time to consider the processes that initiate and sustain desistance.

by the respondents. Savings were quickly exhausted and the culture of addiction justified the use of virtually any means to get money in order to support their habits.

For the majority of women, the problem of maintaining an addiction took precedence over all other interests and over participation in other social worlds. Their primary reference group, people they associated with, was involved in a wide range of illicit behaviors. Over time, the study women became further enmeshed in deviance and further alienated, both socially and psychologically, from conventional life. The women's lives became bereft of conventional involvements, obligations, and responsibilities. The excitement of the lifestyle that may have characterized their early criminal career phase gave way to a much more serious and grave daily existence.

The following accounts illustrate the uncertainty and vulnerability of street life. Denise, a 33-year-old Black woman participated in a wide range of street crimes including burglary, robbery, assault, and drug dealing. She began dealing drugs when she was 14 and used cocaine on a regular basis by the age of 19.

> I was in a lot of fights. So I had fights over, uh, drugs, or, you know, just manipulation. There's a lot of manipulation in that life. Everybody's tryin' to get over. Everybody will stab you in your back, you know. Nobody gives a fuck about the next person, you know. It's just when you want it, you want it. You know, when you want that drug, you know, you want that drug. There's a lot of lyin', a lot if manipulation. It's, it's, it's crazy! It also got frightening.

Gazella, a 38-year-old Hispanic women, had been involved in crime for 22 years when we interviewed her.

> I'm 34 years old. I ain't no young woman no more, man. Drugs have changed, lifestyles have changed. Kids are killing you now for turf. Yeah, turf, and I was destroyin' myself. I was miserable. I was . . . I was gettin' high all the time to stay up to keep the business going, and it was really nobody I could trust. Things kept getting worse and worse. Everything was spoiling around me.

Sonya, a 27-year-old Hispanic women, provides an account of what daily life was like on the streets.

> You get tired of bein' tired, you know. I got tired of hustlin', you know. I got tired of livin' the way I was livin', you know. Due to your body, your body, mentally, emotionally, you know. Everybody's tryin' to get over. Everybody will stab you in your back. Nobody gives a fuck about the next person. And I used to have people talkin' to me, "you know, you're not a bad lookin' girl. You know, why you don't get yourself together."

Additional illustrations of the exigencies of street-life are provided by April and Stephanie. April was a 25-year-old Black woman at the time of the interview who had been involved in crime since she was 11.

> I wasn't eating. Sometimes I wouldn't eat for two or three days. And I would . . . a lot of times I wouldn't have the time, or I wouldn't want to spend the money to eat -- I've got to use it to get high. My teeth were falling out and I looked real bad. I never knew what was going to happen--whether I would have something to eat, someplace to live, anything.

Stephanie, a 27-year-old Black women, had used and sold crack for five years:

> I knew that, uh, I was gonna get killed out here. I wasn't havin' no respect for myself. No one else was respecting me. Every relationship I got into, as long as I did drugs, it was gonna be constant disrespect involved, and it come . . . to the point of me gettin' killed. I had a few times when I thought that was going to happen--that that was going to be the end of it.

When the "spiral down" finally reached its lowest point, the women reported being overwhelmed by a sense of personal despair. In reporting the early stages of this period of despair, the respondents consistently voiced two themes- the hopeless futility of their lives and their personal isolation. Barbara, a 31-year-old Black woman, began using crack when she was 23. By age 25, Barbara had lost her job at the Board of Education and was involved in burglary and robbery. Her account is typical of the despair the women in our sample eventually experienced:

> The fact that my family didn't trust me anymore, and the way that my daughter was looking at me, and, uh, my mother wouldn't let me in her house anymore, and I was sleepin' on the trains. And I was sleepin' on the beaches in the summertime. And I was really frightened. I was real scared of the fact that I had to sleep on the train. And, uh, I had to wash up in the Port Authority. I was alone and no one was helping me anymore. I used to have

my family when things got real rough. I always thought I would eventually have my daughter. But, I was all of a sudden, all alone.

The effects of the spiral down were also felt by Gazella who was forced to live on the streets.

> It was the first time that I didn't have a place to live. My kids had been taken away from me. You know, constantly being harassed like three days out of the week by the Tactical Narcotics Team (police). I didn't't want to be bothered with people. I was gettin' tired of the lyin', schemin', you know, stayin' in abandoned buildings, runnin', hidin' and all the while looking for more drugs. It was the final thing of living on the streets and all that came with it that did me in. There was no future.

For many of the women, it was the stresses of street life and the fear of dying on the streets that motivated their decision to quit the criminal life. Darlene, a 25-year-old Black woman, recalled the stress associated with the latter stage of her drug selling career.

> The simple fact is that I really, I thought that I would die out there. I thought that someone would kill me out there and I would be killed, I had a fear of being on the front page one day and being in the newspaper dying. I wanted to live, and I didn't just want to exist. But the street didn't let me do either, really. It got to the point where I wasn't even sure that I existed.

Alicia, a 29-year-old Hispanic woman became involved in street violence when she was 12 years old. She comments on the personal isolation that was a consequence of her involvement in crime. In her case, though, the estrangement came from her end:

> When I started getting involved in crime, you know, and drugs, the friends that I had, even my family, I stayed away from them, you know. You know how you look bad and you feel bad, and you just don't want those people to see you like you are. So I avoided seeing them. I didn't want them seeing me that way or knowing how low I got to get the drugs. But, things got real bad on the street. I was totally out there alone. I stopped knowing who I was, really. What happened to the me who had a family?

For some, the emotional depth of the rock-bottom crisis was felt as a sense of mortification. Here, the women felt they had nowhere to turn to salvage a sense of well-being or self-worth. Suicide was considered a better alternative than remaining in such an undesirable social and psychological state. Denise's account was typical of the women who had attempted suicide as a way out of the life:

> I ran into a girl who I went to school with that works on Wall Street. And I compared her life to mine and it was like miserable. Here she had a family, a job, friends. She looked good. She cared about herself. She had people who cared about her. It made me just want out. I was tired, I was run down, looking bad. I thought I could get out, forever, by smashing myself through a sixth-floor window. But I lived. Then I went to the psychiatric ward and I met this real nice doctor, and we talked every day. She fought to keep me in the hospital because she felt I wouldn't survive. She believed in me. And she talked me into going into a drug program.

Marginalization from family, friends, children, legal work, in short, the loss of traditional life structures, left women like Denise feeling hypervulnerable to chaotic street conditions. But for the women in this desistance subsample, the overwhelming sense of despair that had overcome them also led them, eventually, to begin the process of questioning and reevaluating their identities and their social construction of the world.

The women we spoke to repeated over and over that they had grown tired of a life filled with constant pain, terror, distress and severe hardship. Even incarceration came to be viewed as yet another assault, rather than a respite, as some had believed earlier. The bottom line was that they grew tired of the street experiences and the problems and consequences of criminal involvement. This has been an observation commonly made by researchers on male offenders (Cusson and Pinsonneault, 1986; Shover, 1985). It appears as though regardless of gender, with age, the prospect of incurring another prison term becomes more difficult to deal with and affects decisions to desist.

Gazella recalls her last prison term:

> First of all when I was in prison I was like, I was so humiliated. At my age [38] I was really kind of embarrassed, but I knew that was the lifestyle that I was leadin'. And people I used to talk to would tell me well you could do this, and you don't have to get busted. But then I started thinking why are all these people here. So it doesn't, you know, really work. So I came home, and I did go back to selling again, but you know I knew I was on probation. And I didn't want to do no more time. I knew that I wasn't going to survive the next time. I couldn't handle the thought of doing time again.

April, too, grew tired of being confined and anticipated with dread the potential for subsequent incarceration:

> Jail, being in jail. The environment, having my freedom taken away. I saw myself keep repeating the same pattern, and I didn't want to do that. Uh, I had missed my daughter. See, being in jail that long period of time, I was able to detox. And when I detoxed, I kind of like had a clear sense of thinking, and that's when I came to the realization that, uh, this is not working for me. It used to be a place to rest, but the last time was too tough. I felt like I was climbing the walls--that I would never get out alive. If I stayed in this life, I would have ended up again in jail. But, I wouldn't make it out next time. Oh god, I know I couldn't do it again.

Denise had never been incarcerated, but the prospect of it frightened her in a way that she never thought about in the past:

> Oh yeah, people were always going away. Maybe my turn would come one day. That's what I used to think. Then I saw the person that I was dealing with -- my partner -- I saw her go up State to Bedford for two to four years. I didn't want to deal with it. I didn't want to go. Bedford is a prison, women's prison. And I couldn't see myself givin' up two years of my life for something that I knew I could change in another way. I knew it wasn't too late for me and that my luck was probably going to be running out soon too. Never thought about it that way before, but I really am scared of spending the next few years of my life living like my partner.

As we can see, a change in their attitude towards surviving incarceration (which they increasingly viewed as a realistic outcome of their continued involvement in criminal behavior) affected their decisions to desist.

Perhaps even more important, the women felt that they had wasted time. They became acutely aware of time as a diminishing resource (Shover, 1983). The women reported that they saw themselves going nowhere and that they did not have much more time to get on with things. The women arrived at a point where crime seemed senseless and their lives had reached a dead end. Implicit in this assessment was the belief that gaining a longer-range perspective on one's life was a first step in changing. These deliberations developed as a result of "socially disjunctive experiences" which caused the women to experience social stress, feelings of alienation and dissatisfaction with their present identities (Ray, 1961).

BREAKING AWAY FROM THE LIFE

Forming a commitment to change was only the first step toward ending their criminal careers. The women then entered a period which has been characterized as a "running struggle" with problems of social identity (Ray, 1961, p. 136). To be successful at desistance, these women had to work hard at clarifying and strengthening their nondeviant identity, and at redefining their street experiences in terms more compatible with conventional lifestyles. This second stage of desistance required that the women make a public announcement or "certification" (Meisenhelder 1977, p. 329) that she decided to end her criminal involvement. Once accomplished, she must then begin to redefine the economic, social and emotional relationships that had been rooted in the deviant street subculture.

This period was one of ambivalence and crisis. For these women, so much of their lives had revolved around street life. Further, they had, at best, only weak associations with the conventional world. Many of the women remembered the uncertainty they felt and the social dilemmas they faced after they decided to stop their involvement in crime. Denise describes her own situation:

> I went and looked up my old friends and to see what was doing, and my girlfriend Mia was like, she was gettin' paid. And I was livin' on a $60 stipend. And I wasn't with it. Mia was good to me, she always kept money in my pocket when I came home. I would walk into her closet and change into clothes that I'm more accustomed to. She started calling me Pen again. She stopped calling me Denise. And I would ride with her knowing that she had a gun or a package in the car. But I wouldn't touch nothin'. But that was my rationale. As long as I don't fuck with nothin. Yeah, she was like I can give you a grand and get you started. I said I know you can, but I can't. She said I can give you a grand, and she kept telling me that over and over; and I wasn't that far from taking the grand and getting started again. I was confused for a while and it caused me lots of pain.

Barbara also offered an account of her experiences:

> After I decided to change, I went to a party with my friend. And people was around me and they was drinkin' and stuff, and I didn't want to drink. I don't have the urge of drinking. If anything, it would be smokin' crack. And when I left the party, I felt like I was missing something -- like something was missing. And it was the fact that I wasn't gettin' high. But I know the

consequences of it. If I take a drink, I'm gonna smoke crack. If I, uh, sniff some blow, I'm gonna smoke crack. I might do some things like rob a store or something stupid and go to jail. So I don't want to put myself in that position. But it really hurt to not be down with them.

At this stage of their transition, the women had to face some very basic issues. Perhaps foremost was the dilemma about what to do with themselves and their lives. Furthermore, they were clueless in terms of how to establish and maintain conventional relationships. Few of the women had maintained their ties to people who were not involved in crime and drugs. And, given their family histories, few had past experiences from which to model. Given this situation, the women had to work hard in order to construct alternatives to their deviant social worlds.

The large majority of the women were aided in their social reintegration by help that was outside of their social worlds. The women perceived clearly the need to remove themselves from the "scene", to meet new friends and to begin the process of identity reformation. Often, they sought formal treatment of some kind as a way of removing themselves from the ever present and overpowerful deviant social world. Typically, they entered residential drug treatment programs that provided them with structure, social support, and a pathway to behavioral change. The following account by Alicia typifies the importance of a "geographic cure."

> I love to get high. You know, and I love the way crack makes me feel. I knew that I needed long-term, I knew that I needed to go somewhere. All away from everything, and I just needed to be away from everything. And I couldn't deal with responsibility at all. And, uh, I was just so ashamed of the way that I had, you know, became and the person that I became that I just wanted to start over again. But it wasn't going to happen if I stayed in the same place. I had to get away from the pull.

Social avoidance strategies were a common thread in all of their attempts at desistance. Clearly, they recognized that their continued involvement in crime and drugs would be made more difficult if they removed themselves from their old social worlds and old locations. April discussed this with us:

> Yeah, I go home, but I don't, I don't socialize with the people. I don't even speak to anybody really. I go and I come. I don't go to the areas that I used to be in. I don't go there anymore. I don't walk

> down the same blocks I used to walk down. I always take different locations. I avoid those people and sometimes, I know that I can't even go home if I am feeling weak. I need that space away from those influences. Anyway, they'll forget about me if I'm not around and I'll lose those connections if I stay away long enough. That's what I have to do to stay out of the life.

Denise, too acknowledges the importance of maintaining distance from her old world:

> I miss the fast money; otherwise, I don't miss my old life. I get support from my positive friends, and in the program. I talk about how I felt being around my old associates, seeing them, you know, going back to my old neighborhood. It's hard to deal with, I have to push away. I have to stay away. That way, I can keep strong and give up on the fast money. Being away helps me remember how low I got and how the fast money didn't buy me a life. As lone as I stay away, I can keep clear of those things.

MAINTAINING A CONVENTIONAL LIFE

Most of these women have little chance of staying "out of the life" for an extended period of time if they stay in the social world of crime and addiction. Instead, they must build and *maintain* a network of primary relations who accept and support their nondeviant identity. This third stage of desistance is essential if they are to be successful. Surely, this is no easy task. Desisters have in most cases alienated their old nondeviant primary relations.

But, these women worked hard at maintaining the straight and narrow. They were like religious converts in terms of the fervor with which they attempted to establish and maintain support networks that validated their new sense of self. This was facilitated by their participation in treatment programs.

Generally, treatment programs provide both a ready-made primary group for the desister, but also a well established *pervasive identity* (Travisano 1970). Thus, being an ex-con and/or an ex-addict continually informed the women's view of herself in a variety of interactions. Reminders of "spoiled identities" (Goffman 1963) such as criminal, ex-con, ex-junkie serve as constant reference points for new experiences. Further, they help maintain the saliency of conventional living (Faupel 1991). Perhaps most important in terms of treatment programs is the simple fact that they provided the women with an alternative basis for life structure- one that was devoid of crime, drugs and other subcultural elements.

The successful treatment program, however, is one that ultimately facilitates dissociation and promotes independent living. Dissociation from programs to participate in conventional living requires association, or reintegration with conventional society. For the study women, friends, educational and occupational roles developed within the context of these treatment programs helped to reaffirm their noncriminal identities and bond them to conventional lifestyles. Barbara describes the assistance she received from friends and from her treatment groups:

> The program has given me a bunch of friends that always confronts me on what I'm doin', and where I'm goin', and they just want the best for me. And none of them use drugs. I go to a lot like outside support groups, you know. They help me have more confidence in myself. I have new friends now. Some of them are in treatment. Some have always been straight. They know. You know, they glad, you know, when I see them. They're always there for me and, I'm learning to be there for them. I feel like I belong, that there is a place for me with them. It is really great that straight people even accept me.

In the course of experiencing relationships with conventional others and participating in conventional roles, the women developed a strong social-psychological commitment not to return to crime and drug use. These commitments were often strengthened by renewed affiliations with their children, relationships with new friends, and the acquisition of educational and vocational skills.

The social relationships, interests, and investments that developed in the course of desistance reflected the gradual emergence of their new identities. Such stakes in conventional identity form the social-psychological context within which control and desistance were possible (Waldorf, et al. 1991). In short, the women developed a stake in their new lives that was incompatible with street life. These new stakes served as wedges to help maintain the separation of the women from the world of the streets (Biernacki 1986).

This desire to maintain one's sense of self was an important incentive for avoiding return to crime. As Alicia recounts:

> I like the fact that I have my respect back. I like the fact that, uh, my daughter trusts me again. And my mother don't mind leavin' me in the house,

and she don't have to worry that when she come in her TV might be gone. I feel real good about this.

Barbara, too, takes great pride in her new self identify:

> I have new friends. I have my children back in my life. I have my education. It keeps me straight. I can't forget where I came from because I get scared to go back. I don't want to go back. I don't want to hurt nobody. I just want to live a normal life. It has been tough, but look what I have in return--my family, great friends who love me for who I really am, a future. It was a long road, but I'm not turning back.

But, for some, the tension between staying straight and returning to the deviant street scene is tremendous. Janelle, a 22-year-old Black woman, started dealing drugs and carrying a 38-caliber gun when she was 15. She describes this ongoing tension:

> It's hard, it's hard stayin' on the right track. But lettin' myself know that I'm worth more helps. I don't have to go in a store today and steal anything. I don't deserve that. I don't deserve to make myself feel really bad. Then once again I would be steppin' back and feel that this is all I can do. I feel like I'm being pulled between these two worlds and I am not sure where I will fit in. I guess it will all depend on what's comfortable.

Overall, the way to an identity transformation hinged on the women's abilities to establish and maintain commitments and involvements in conventional aspects of life. As the women began to feel accepted and trusted within some conventional social circles their determination to exit from crime was strengthened as was their social and personal identities as noncriminals. Their "comfort" with their new identities was crucial to maintaining the desistance process.

THE DESISTANCE PROCESS

Desistance is a process as complex and lengthy as the processes of initial involvement. It was interesting to find that some of the key concepts in initiation of deviance- social bonding, differential association, deterrence, age- were equally important in the process of desistance. We see the aging offender take the threat of punishment seriously, reestablish links with conventional society, and sever associations with subcultural street elements.

We found, too, that the decision to give up crime was triggered by a shock of some sort that was followed by a period of crisis. Anxious and dissatisfied they took stock of their lives and criminal activity. The women arrived at a point where the deviant way of life seemed senseless. Having made this assessment, the women then worked to clarify and strengthen their nondeviant identities. This phase began with the reevaluation of life goals and the public announcement of their decision to end their involvement in crime. Once the decision to quit was made, the women turned to (or created new) relationships that had not been ruined by their deviance. The final stage, maintaining cessation, involved integration into a nondeviant lifestyle. This meant restructuring the entire pattern of their lives (i.e., primary relationships, daily routines, social situations). For most women, treatment groups provided the continuing support to maintain a nondeviant status.

The change processes and turning points described by the women were quite similar to those reported by men in previous studies (Shover, 1983, 1985; Cusson and Pinsonneault 1986). Basically, turning points occur as a "part of a process over time and not as a dramatic lasting change that takes place at any one time" (Pickles and Rutter 1991, p. 134). Thus, the return to conventional life occurs more because of "push" rather than "pull" factors (Adler 1992). This appears to be due to result from a point of time in the criminal career when involvement in crime moves offenders beyond the point at which s/he finds it enjoyable to the point at which it is debilitating and anxiety provoking.

Clearly, these interviews are limited in terms of their generalizability. Yet, there are some important ideas that emerged from this group of women who were deeply involved in crime and immersed in a street subculture yet who found the strength and resources to change their lives. At the same time, the fact that all of the women who quit their involvement in crime experienced a long period of personal deterioration and a "rock bottom" experience before they were able to exit, does not mean that all who hit that point will stop or that this is the only process by which offenders will desist. There are undoubtedly other scenarios. There is always the case of the occasional offender who will forever drift in and out of crime; there is the offender who stops when criminal involvement threatens and conflicts with commitments to conventional life; or there is the battered woman who kills only once, in response to her abusive situation- in this instance, the question of desistance does not arise.

Figure 1: The Desistance Process

Stage 1 Problems associated with criminal participation

Socially Disjunctive Experiences	Delayed Deterrence
hitting rock bottom	increased probability of punishment
fear of death	increased difficulty in "doing time"
tiredness	increased severity of sanctions
illness	increasing fear

Assessment
reappraisal of life and goals
psychic change

Decision
Decision to quit and/or initial attempts at desistance
Continuing possibility of criminal participation

Stage 2 Restructuring of Self

- Public pronouncement of decision to end criminal participation
- Claim to a new social identity

Stage 3 Maintenance of the Decision to Stop

- Ability to successfully renegotiate identity
- Support of significant others
- Integration into new social networks
- Ties to Conventional roles
- Stabilization of new social identity

Nevertheless, the experiences of these women offer useful perspectives for thinking about a theory of cessation. Drawing upon their accounts as well as on common themes in the literature on exiting or "quitting" deviant careers, we present a model for understanding desistance from crime (Figure 1). Three stages characterize the cessation process: building resolve or discovering motivation to stop (i.e., socially disjunctive experiences), making and publicly disclosing the decision to stop, and maintenance of the new behaviors and integration into new social networks (Stall and Biernacki 1986; Mulvey and Aber 1988). These phases resemble the cessation processes described by Waldorf et al. (1991, p. 240) in their study of cocaine quitters. They describe three ideal-typical phases of desistance: "turning points" where offenders begin consciously to experience negative effects (socially disjunctive experiences); "active quitting" where they take steps to exit crime (public pronouncement); and "maintaining cessation" (identity transformation).

Stage 1: Catalysts for Change

When external conditions change and reduce the "rewards of deviant behavior," motivation may build to end criminal involvement. That process, and the resulting decision, seem to be associated with two related conditions: a series of negative, aversive, unpleasant experiences from criminal behavior, or, corollary situations where the positive rewards, status, or gratification from crime are reduced. Shover and Thompson's (1992) research suggests that the probability of desistance from criminal participation increases as expectations for achieving rewards (e.g., friends, money, autonomy) via crime decreases and that changes in expectations are age-related.

Shover (1983) contends that the daily routines of managing criminal involvement become tiring and burdensome to aging offenders. Consequently, the allure of crime diminishes as offenders get older. Aging may also increase the perceived formal risk of criminal participation. Cusson and Pinsonneault (1986, p. 76) point out that "with age, criminals raise their estimates of the certainty of punishment." Fear of reimprisonment, fear of longer sentences, and the increasing difficulty of "doing time" has often been reported by investigators who have explored desistance.

Stage 2: Discontinuance

The second stage of the model begins with the public announcement that the offender has decided to end their criminal participation. Such an announcement forces the start of a process of renegotiation of the offender's social identity (Stall and Biernacki 1986). After this announcement, the offender must not only cope with the instrumental aspects (e.g., financial) of her life but must also begin to redefine important emotional and social relationships that are influenced or predicated upon criminal behavior.

Leaving a deviant subculture is difficult. Biernacki (1986) noted the exclusiveness of the social involvements maintained by former addicts during initial stages of abstinence. With social embedment comes the gratification of social acceptance and social identity. The decision to end a behavior that is socially determined and supported implies withdrawal of the social gratification it brings. Thus, the more deeply embedded in a criminal social context, the more dependent the offender is on that social world for her primary sources of approval and social definition.

The responses by social control agents, family members, and peer supporters to further criminal participation are critical to shaping the outcome of discontinuance. New social and emotional worlds to replace the old ones may strengthen the decision to stop. Adler (1992) found that outside associations and involvements provided a critical bridge back into society for dealers who decided to leave the drug subculture. With discontinuance comes the difficult work of identity transformations (Biernacki 1986) and establishing new social definitions of behavior and relationships to reinforce them.

Stage 3: Maintenance

Following the initial stages of discontinuance, strategies to avoid a return to crime build on the strategies to first break from a lengthy pattern of criminal participation: further integration into a non-criminal identity and social world and maintaining the costs of criminal participation. Maintenance depends in part on replacing deviant networks of peers and associates with supports which both sanction criminal participation and approve of new non-deviant beliefs. Treatment interventions (e.g., drug treatment, social service programs) are important sources of alternative social supports to maintain a noncriminal lifestyle. In other words, maintenance depends on immersion into a social world where criminal behavior meets immediately with strong formal and informal sanctions. Despite these efforts to maintain non-criminal involvement, desistance is likely to be episodic, with occasional bouts interspersed with lengthening of lulls.

Cessation is part of a social-psychological transformation for the offender. A strategy to stabilize the transition to a non criminal lifestyle requires the active use of supports to maintain the norms which have been substituted for the forces which supported criminal behavior in the past.

Chapter 8

CONCLUSIONS

In the preceding chapters, we have described how the development of a cocaine economy created opportunities for drug selling that did not exist in the smaller, more stable heroin markets. The changing social and economic structures of inner city neighborhoods also created the possibility of changes in the gender roles that, in the past, constrained women's options for status and income within street drug networks. At one time, women were excluded from selling by rigid gender roles and male hegemony in deviant street networks. The expanding cocaine economy neutralized these social processes that in the past consigned them to secondary roles in street networks. The combination of these factors enabled women either to circumvent gender roles in street drug networks and form new drug selling organizations, or pursue independent careers in drug selling.

The data examined in this book reaffirm the importance of social factors in accounting for criminal career patterns. The results suggest that initiation into drug dealing for the 156 study women was strongly influenced by the neighborhood environment. These women came from two of the most severely distressed communities in New York City where the stresses of poverty and the increases in illegal opportunities combined with a weakening in the social control capabilities of neighborhood institutions. Thus, these women grew up in multiproblem households where the absence of conventional role models, social support and material resources weakened the socialization functions of the family. They experienced detachment from such conventional institutions as school, marriage and employment, and by adulthood, most were deeply entrenched in substance abuse and related deviant lifestyles.

The growing concentration of poverty, joblessness and family disruption has signaled a transformation in the social and institutional structure of the inner city. In turn, there has been a general weakening in the structures of economic opportunities and processes of social sanctions that mediate the development of social and economic capital for inner city residents. Neighborhood change has weakened formal and informal social controls, and the material and social rewards for legal behavior have all but disappeared.

Our research suggests that these processes, so often identified as criminogenic in terms of inner city males, affects women living in these communities, as well. For both men and women in a changing economy, filling the market niche for drug products or other illegal goods is a logical entrepreneurial response, particularly when the historical avenues to labor market participation have been truncated by the restructuring of the city and regional economy. The informal economy grew disproportionately in the 1980s in New York neighborhoods with high concentrations of poor, minority populations (Sassen-Koob, 1989), and drug selling has always been an important part of the informal economy (Fagan, 1992). The growth in drug use and the rapid expansion of the cocaine and crack markets in the 1980s created a complex drug industry, albeit one that functioned outside formal (legal) systems of regulation and that relied on violence for its maintenance. Drawn by the promise of high profits with minimal capital investment, drug sellers became suppliers of important goods and services to both local markets and residents of more affluent areas (Sullivan, 1989). Thus, the vitality of a drug market in a neighborhood is bound up with the relationships within poor neighborhoods and between these neighborhoods and other parts of their cities. To the extent that women's roles and prominence have changed in transformed neighborhoods, their involvement in drug selling and other crimes that include street violence reflects the dynamics of the neighborhoods themselves.

The results also suggest variation among the study women. The findings demonstrate that individual level factors related to onset of drug selling change as youths age through adolescence and young adulthood. On the one hand, early initiation into drug dealing was accompanied by participation in a wide variety of other offending behaviors and deviant lifestyles. On the other hand, those women who experienced a later onset of dealing did so within the context of a criminal career that, up to the point of substance abuse, was more specialized and focused on typically nonviolent, gender congruent activities (e.g., prostitution, shoplifting).

While our focus has been on the role of structural dislocation, community context, and opportunity structure in shaping the life course, the analyses presented here do not imply that the women had no choice nor do they attempt to absolve the women from responsibility for their actions but claim only to indicate that, under certain conditions and in certain contexts, some women are more likely than not to choose to be involved in illegal enterprises.

The societal response to crime problems arguably borne from social and economic conditions has been the traditional "crackdown," rooted in deterrence and punishment theories. The anti-crime crusades of the 1980s have translated into laws and policies that rely heavily on law enforcement efforts and criminal sanctions, especially incarceration. We conclude with a discussion of how New York's justice system confronted the problems of drug trafficking and use.

CRIMINAL SANCTIONS AND DRUG MARKETS

The devastation of the crack era, on the communities and lives of these women cannot be underestimated. But these words echo from past eras. Since the 1880s, social and legal responses to successive drug crises have reacted to each new drug as though it were different and more severe than its predecessors. In each instance, policies were developed within the context of moral crusades (Gusfield, 1975; Reinerman and Levine, 1989) to mobilize legal institutions to control the use of the targeted intoxicants. Responses to marijuana in the 1930s and again in the 1960s (Silver, 1979), heroin in the 1960s and 1970s (Epstein, 1977; Kaplan, 1983; Trebach, 1982), PCP in the late 1970s (Feldman, Agar, & Beschner, 1979), and several cocaine crises in the 1980s (Office of National Drug Control Policy, 1989 [hereafter, ONDCP, 1989]; Zimmer, 1987; Zimring & Hawkins, 1992) regarded the drug of the day as a gateway to violence, addiction, and a variety of destructive effects on families and communities.

Throughout each of these crises, law and policy have increasingly relied on criminal sanctions to control drug use and drug selling. In September 1989, the publication of the *National Drug Control Strategy*, formalized the nation's policy response to the most recent drug crisis (ONDCP, 1989). It called for an "unprecedented" expansion of police, prosecutors, courts, and prisons to "[make] streets safer and drug users more accountable for their actions" (ONDCP, p. 24). It also called for stronger punishment for drug offenders, and greater resolve by judges and prosecutors to incarcerate them.

By stating drug problems in *moral* terms, or *mala in se* (Hughes, 1983), the ONDCP policy defines drug use and selling as dual problems of legal transgressions. First, the ONDCP policy assumes that all drugs are bad, and that none is more dangerous than any other. Taking or selling illegal drugs is a socially deviant act whose social and health consequences are sufficiently harmful to merit state control and intervention. Second, because drugs are illegal, taking or selling them undermines the law and, by extension, the social order of laws.' Every illegal drug user has violated societal norms and must be held accountable for doing so.

These assumptions fueled a mobilization of legal and political institutions throughout the past decade and repeated a cycle that has been evident in American social and political life for more than a century (Myers, 1989; Reinarman & Levine, 1989). For example, police crackdowns on street-level drug trafficking have been widely implemented since the mid-1970s (Chaiken, 1988; Moore, 1977; Sherman, 1990). By 1982, a cycle of congressional activism began, which lengthened prison sentences and made incarceration mandatory for specific federal offenses, placed restrictions on bail, and limited the use of the exclusionary rule (Zimring & Hawkins, 1992).

States quickly followed suit. In 1985, Georgia legislation increased mandatory minimum sentences for cocaine trafficking, permitted fines up to $500,000, and restricted judicial discretion in sentencing. New Jersey's 1987 drug legislation, considered a "model for the nation" (New Jersey Supreme Court, 1990), mandated imprisonment for selling drugs within 1,000 feet of a school, and increased penalties for all drug possession and sale offenses. In 1988, New York legislators reduced the threshold for a felony cocaine possession charge from one-eighth ounce (3.5 grams) to approximately one gram, or six vials of crack. Penalties for felony sale convictions were set equal to mandatory minimums for armed robbery, aggravated assault, and manslaughter. Both New York and Georgia passed laws mandating incarceration for second drug convictions. These statutes typified legislative efforts to strengthen punishment and increase its certainty.

One obvious result of the war on drugs has been vast increases in drug arrests, both for possession and selling, and a dramatic change in the composition of defendant and prison populations. Between 1980 and 1988, drug arrests in New York City increased from 18,521 (40% for heroin or other opiates) to 88,641 (44% for crack) (Belenko, Fagan, & Chin, 1991). The proportion of drug arrestees increased from 11 % of the arrestee population in 1980 to 31% in 1989 (New York City Police Department, 1990).

Drug arrestees have also received harsher treatment at all stages of case processing, compared with both non-drug arrestees and drug arrestees during earlier drug epidemics. Since 1983, drug offenders in New York City have a higher probability of felony charges at arrest, are less likely to make bail, and are more likely to be held in pretrial detention without bail (Belenko et al., 1991). In the courts, drug caseloads increased by 56% between 1983 and 1987 in a sample of 26 cities nationwide (Goerdt & Martin, 1989).

In New York, California, and the federal prison systems, drug offenders are now the largest inmate group (Bureau of Justice Statistics, 1992). In the federal prisons in 1990, more than 50% of the 1990 inmates were drug offenders (BJS, 1992). In 1988, drug offenders comprised more than 20% of New York State prison population, exceeding all other offense and offender types and outpacing rapid prison expansion (Division of Criminal Justice Services [hereafter, DCJS], 1988); within one year, drug offenders comprised more than one third of the prison inmates (DCJS, 1990). In California, 43% of the admissions to state prison were parole violators returned to prison by the Parole Board without a conviction for a new charge, due in large part to the increased use of drug testing by parole officers (Messinger et al., 1988). This situation was evident in other large states nationwide, including Texas and Florida (BJS, 1989). As investments in treatment and other sentencing alternatives have lagged behind the growth in arrests and convictions, prison populations have grown sharply.

Obviously, efforts to mobilize legal institutions to respond more harshly to drug crimes have been successful. Arrests, prosecutions, convictions, prison sentences, and parole revocations all have increased sharply in a relatively short time (Zimring and Hawkins, 1992). Both legislative activism and the political salience of drug cases increased the likelihood that drug offenders would be incarcerated, regardless of their criminal histories or the comparative risks they posed to public safety (Belenko et al., 1991).

Women have been affected adversely by these punitive policies. Female populations in jails and prisons have increased dramatically. The United States Bureau of Justice Statistics (BJS) reports that the average daily population of women confined in local jails rose by 95.3 percent between 1984 and 1989. The number of men in jail increased by 51 percent during this period. Overall, between 1980 and 1989, arrests for drug abuse violations increased 176% for females v. 118% for males (U.S. Department of Justice, 1990).

And, looking at New York State corrections data, we detect further evidence of the impact of the "war on drugs". From January, 1987 through December, 1989, drug commitments to state prison for females rose 211 percent--and for males, the increase was 82 percent (New York State Department of Correctional Services, 1990). Over this three year period, 77 percent of female drug offenders were incarcerated for sale, as opposed to possession, of a controlled substance. Furthermore, while the proportion of the male commitment population imprisoned for drug offenses rose from 32 percent in 1987 to 44 percent in 1989, the growth in female drug commitments has been even more striking. It increased from 42 percent of the 1987 court commitment population to 66 percent in 1989.

MOBILIZING THE LAW FOR DETERRENCE

The mobilization of the criminal law to deter drug crimes has both symbolic and substantive components. Certainly, the passage of legislative mandates for lengthy prison terms "symbolizes public contempt for the actions of persons who sell, manufacture, or possess large quantities of drugs" (Myers, 1989, p. 296). Such responses are particularly appropriate when drug use is defined as a "moral problem" (ONDCP 1989, P. 53). The symbolic component of drug policy may be intended as a general deterrent, by conveying the message that legal consequences are likely and severe if one uses or sells drugs.

However, no such clarity is evident regarding the substantive bases of criminal punishment for drug offenders. Apart from conveying societal outrage at drug offenders, we expect the law to "do something" about drug problems. Yet the intent of the criminal law and the precise meaning of criminal sanctions is rarely stated with such precision. Although federal policy calls for the use of "tough and coherently punitive anti-drug measures"

(ONDCP, 1989, p. 5) that call for more police and more prisons (ONDCP, cited in Zimring & Hawkins, 1992), we are not told why criminal sanctions are appropriate: to retributively punish drug offenders, to incapacitate them, or to deter them from further involvement with drugs.

The substantive component evidently is a specific deterrent: to stop people from using drugs, to stop users who are "highly contagious" (ONDCP, 1989, p. 8). Such laws may also reflect incapacitative intents: The ONDCP strategy mentions "a short-term reduction in the number of ... casual and regular users" and "future reductions in [those who] are recruited" (ONDCP, 1989, p. 7). In either view, the use of criminal sanctions is intended to reduce the extent and severity of drug problems by incarcerating drug offenders.

DETERRENCE AND THE ECONOMIC CONTEXT OF SANCTIONS

As we have argued, the expansion of the drug economy in the 1980s created opportunities for income and drug use that have been well exploited by both female and male inner-city residents. Participants in drug use and selling were people who were not well matched to the rapidly changing formal labor market, either spatially or in their job skills (Case & Katz, 1990; Fagan, 1992; Freeman, 1991). And, they were very well matched to the labor market for drug distribution (Fagan & Chin, 1990). However, drug selling did not draw people away from the formal labor market (Fagan, 1992), yet, for many already employed, drug selling offered greater rewards (but with greater risks) than formal income.

Although the women sellers we studied, acknowledged the legal, physical, and social risks of their work, criminal punishment was not high among them. The risk of physical harm was more salient for this group than arrest or incarceration. Freeman (1991) and Reuter (1990) found similar trends for risk assessments and the deterrent effects of perceived sanctions among disadvantaged inner-city youths in Boston and Washington, D.C., respectively. Fagan (1992) and Padilla (1992) showed the strong economic incentives for drug selling compared to licit income among young drug sellers, and the independence of drug selling from prior incarceration experiences.

For the women outside the formal and/or licit economy, the high returns from drug selling raised their reservation wage (the base wage at which they will enter the formal labor market) and further distanced them from legal economic activities (Bluestone, Stevenson, & Tilly, 1991; Moss & Tilly, 1991). For participants in the illicit economy of drug selling, punishment was an opportunity cost (i.e., lost income); but so was participation in the formal economy at relatively lower wages (Fagan, 1992). For punishment-imprisonment or probation supervision-to be an effective deterrent, it must be coupled with changes in the perceived marginal gains from continued drug selling, compared to licit economic activities.

Accordingly, the deterrent effects of criminal sanctions are likely to vary with labor market conditions generally, and with specific individuals' positions within the licit or illicit labor market. Stephanie's view of the deterrent effects of incarceration was typical of the women we interviewed:

> It's like a revolving door. I'm comin' in, but then I know that I'm gettin' out. There's always a chance of gettin' caught, right, but there's not much risk. You know what I"m sayin'. I had the upper hand.

Hernimia expressed a similar view:

> All my arrests were for the sale of drugs and possession of drugs. The first time they released me on ROR. I went right back to the streets. The second time, I was in Rikers for only a few days, The third time it was for six months. Then, uh, my sister bailed me out. You it's like you get to a point that... well I was never really actually scared of anything. It's like jail, what the fuck. I didn't really give a shit.

The anti-drug crusades of the 1980s translated into laws and policies that relied heavily on criminal sanctions, especially incarceration, to control the use and trafficking of illicit drugs. Sentences for drug offenders in New York City between 1983 and 1990 reflected ideological trends that regarded punishment as important symbolic and substantive components of anti-drug sentiment. The enactment and popularization of laws mandating incarceration, regardless of their enforcement, symbolized public contempt for both users and sellers (Myers, 1989), while the mobilization of legal institutions to punish drug offenders reflected public will to wage war against drug users.

Whatever the successes of the symbolic component of drug policy, its specific deterrent effects evidently were quite limited for drug offenders in the large and active drug markets in New York in the 1980s. The limited effects of incarceration for all types of drug offenders call into question the assumptions about punishment that mandate or encourage prisons

DETERRENCE AND THE ECONOMETRICS OF DRUG SELLING

The high rate of incarceration suggests that the risk component of deterrence was well implemented in New York; yet offenders were not sensitive to these sanctions. Experienced offenders in particular seemed unfazed by punishment. For them, punishment is likely an accepted hazard of their chosen work that is inconsequential compared to the potential yields of drug crimes.

This raises doubts about the implied econometric model of specific deterrence that does not consider nonlegal factors. As long as demand for drugs remains high, and the likelihood of marginal gains from drug selling are sufficient to neutralize motivations to avoid crime or participate in licit work, offenders in socially and economically marginal neighborhoods may continue to perceive strong economic benefits from participation in the drug economy. They also are likely to perceive little threat of punishment because there are few costs attached to its consequences. That is, their decisions may be independent of the certainty of punishment or its costs if no other choices are perceived. Deterrent effects reflect more than actual or perceived risks-marginal risk and marginal gain from avoidance of risk also are factors that some individuals seem to weigh in deciding that prison is not a threat worth avoiding.

DETERRENCE AND DRUG MARKETS:
THE CASE OF BUSHWICK, BROOKLYN

Heroin and cocaine distribution in the northern tier of Brooklyn was dominated by Puerto Ricans from the early 1960s to the mid 1980s. These hierarchically organized businesses were almost always found operating on the streets. Distributors and consumers found each other with relative ease, but the business was done in full view of other community residents who were generally powerless to alter the situation. By the mid-1980s, Dominicans had begun to make inroads into the drug business in these neighborhoods, especially through their influence in the cocaine business, and quickly replaced Puerto Ricans as the dominant force in the market.

The displacement of Puerto Ricans from ownership positions and the tendency of Dominican-owned businesses to employ other Dominicans (especially in managerial positions) rather than other Latinos or non-Latinos, earned them considerable resentment among rank and file drug business workers.

The street-level drug businesses which were prominent in northern Brooklyn throughout the 1980s operated on a two-tiered system much like the economies discussed in segmented labor market theory: a core of "good" jobs existed for a privileged few, while the majority were consigned to low-wage, high-risk, dead-end jobs. The drug distribution careers of managers were markedly different from that of street-level sellers. Whereas managers could advance through the ranks (there was clearly a hierarchy among managers) and enjoyed some degree of mobility in the sense that they could often move from site to site as a manager, street-level workers found it difficult to advance to the managerial level and most businesses had little interest in moving workers around. This further restricted the career options available to street-level workers.

By the early 1990s, street-level drug markets began to contract into several drug supermarkets. These supermarkets were generally found in neighborhoods where street-level markets had long histories -- those where heroin had been the dominant drug. One outcome of this concentration of drug markets into fewer neighborhoods was that the blatancy and visibility of the market brought increased pressure from various branches of law enforcement. For example, between 1988-92, 8,168 arrests were made in Bushwick by the Police Department's Narcotics Divisions. The turnover of street-level workers forced local drug businesses to recruit and hire from a larger pool of potential distributors (including, Blacks, Whites and women) rather than from the restricted pool of their friends and associates. The separation and estrangement between Dominican owners and non-Dominican labor was further exacerbated by the continued police presence. Owners and managers found that problems with street-level workers were nearly as troublesome as the threat from the police. Part-time employees who were willing to sell drugs during particularly risky hours were clearly aware that the compensation they received (10% profits) was far outweighed by the likelihood of arrest. Many part-time employees felt justified in absconding with product after working through difficult periods of time with little compensation from management. The tendency of part-time employees to abscond with unsold product became as much a problem for street-level drug businesses as the seizure of their product by law enforcement officials. One result of this trend among part-time workers was that their activities were more closely scrutinized by managers. Managers often stayed in the 'shadows' or inside local stores and they demanded that workers stay within their sight. However, despite increased monitoring by managers, many workers managed to slip away even though physical punishment was an expected outcome of absconding with the product. Even with their will-deserved reputations for violence against employees, most local drug businesses had little difficulty in finding drug users to work for them, but they also had little success in keeping workers from absconding with product if given the opportunity.

The initial effects of intensified police efforts to crack down on street-level drug supermarkets were not immediately visible. Heroin, cocaine and crack continued to be available from a large number of street-level distributors, and consumers continued to come to places like Bushwick from around the New York City metropolitan region. As noted above, however, the drug business had begun to change in some fundamental ways. There was a growing rift between management and labor. Management was becoming more insulated from the streets and less concerned about their workers or working conditions. Mounting business losses due to police seizures and/or worker theft saw managers being held accountable for productivity and profits, and they, in turn, placed increased pressure on workers to toe the line. Much of the market violence during this period was directly attributable to these changes in working conditions.

The experience of street-level drug market in Bushwick was perhaps typical of this period. In September 1992, a new Police Department initiative began in Bushwick which involved the combination of frequent Tactical Narcotics Team (TNT) buy-and-bust operations, a heavy saturation of uniformed officers from other Brooklyn precincts, and a variety of other short- and long-term tactics intended to put additional pressure on the largest street-level drug markets. For example, mounted police were stationed in a nearby park where there was a considerable amount of blatant trafficking. A mobile trailer served as a base of operations for additional uniformed officers in the park and on each corner of drug 'hot spots' in the area. Police officers stopped and questioned all pedestrians on these blocks and asked for identification and destination. Non-residents were told to stay out of the area. The heaviest drug trafficking streets were blocked with police vans, diverting vehicles to other streets. When evening came, large flood-lit flat-bed trucks were brought to strategic corners to illuminate entire blocks. Helicopters gave additional support to officers pursuing suspects on foot.

There were various responses from the many drug businesses in the neighborhood. Some of the larger businesses which already had outlets in other neighborhoods simply shifted the majority of their business to these other marketplaces. For example, one large crack and heroin business run by Dominicans shifted their operations to other outlets that they had already established in Brooklyn and Manhattan. Ethnographic observations in Manhattan confirmed that many of the street-level functionaries from this organization were relocated to Spanish Harlem.

Smaller organizations whose members were recruited from outside of Bushwick (e.g., a group of African-Americans from Bedford-Stuyvesant), found no place to conceal their street-level activities. These organizations, whose members were once somewhat concealed by the bustle of the streets in Bushwick, were forced to move out of the neighborhood to more remote and "tougher" Brooklyn neighborhoods, like Brownsville and East New York.

Yet many businesses stayed and explored ways of adapting to this increased pressure. This particularly true for long-standing businesses whose members lived in the neighborhood (family-based businesses or culture-based), but who had no outlets in other neighborhoods. Some managers attempted to reduce the rate of their workers being arrested by employing people who did not fit the prototypical description of a drug seller. Females and persons who looked like panhandlers were aggressively recruited by managers during this period. Yet recruiting people who were not intimately tied into the business was risky; they were likely to abscond with the product if not closely watched by managers.

Other businesses constructed wrought iron enclosures around the stoops of buildings to protect their workers. Drug sellers would stand inside the enclosures and sell through the iron bars. If police officers attempted to arrest them, locked gates delayed the officers long enough for the dealers to escape out the back or over the roof. This technique was short-lived, as police officers quickly blocked the various escape routes used by distributors.

The two methods most frequently employed by those businesses which continued to sell drugs in Bushwick during this period were: 1) selling only to known clients in semi-concealed spots and 2) selling in areas away from the main drug marketplaces. Selling only to known clients changed the market in a fairly dramatic manner. Distributors no longer attracted customers by calling out the brand name of their product from street corners or the stoops of buildings. Instead, they stood in the doorways of bodegas or in the lobbies of buildings and waited for clients to seek them out.

Other street-level drug businesses in Bushwick moved their operations slightly off the main drug selling locations. The marketplace, formerly concentrated within a four block area, became diffused over a much larger territory. Street-level sellers had to remain visible so that customers, who cruised the neighborhood after their former buying spots were overrun with uniformed officers, could spot them. Soon, police, especially TNT, began to target these outlying spots, although it was difficult for them to chase after businesses which shifted their site from day to day. In this manner, they were able to continue operating in the neighborhood with a minimum loss of personnel and/or product.

Within a year of this stepped up police presence, the market began to settle back into a routine. In addition to police pressures, a growing intolerance in the neighborhood toward blatant street-level sales and to the use of those substances by local youth had prompted the remaining businesses in the neighborhood to adapt their operations in several significant ways. What had once been a raucous meeting place of anonymous buyers and sellers was replaced by a new type of market which was almost entirely based inside of bodegas. The move to indoor locations meant that fewer operatives were needed to run the businesses effectively. No longer did local businesses employ large numbers of unreliable, addicted laborers. In many instances, as businesses downsized, transactions with customers were increasingly handled by trustworthy junior level managers. To insulate these valued core employees, businesses began to form paid lookout networks. Lookouts used several tactics to detect and warn colleagues of impending trouble: they stood in front of indoor business locations, they watched out of apartment windows, they stood watch on rooftops, and they rode bicycles around the neighborhood in search of law enforcement personnel.

Behind the counter sales in bodegas were made only to people who were known to the few remaining distributors. Well-known clients became key figures in this marketplace. Outsiders were forced to rely on them as intermediaries to provide access to sequestered distributors and to provide critical information about product quality. To insure that sales remained brisk, however, businesses cultivated relationships with intermediaries. Many local businesses dispatched "salespeople" to visit these influential clients in shooting galleries and crack houses, and give them free samples of the latest product. Sometimes, salespeople from several businesses would meet in these locations and vie for customers. Relationships between salespeople were usually cordial in these settings since any violent incident was likely to attract the attention of the police and bring additional unwanted scrutiny to their businesses. To avoid arrest, salespeople often avoided bringing samples with them into these settings. Instead, they would give out printed vouchers which contained the location of the distribution spot and a serial number to prevent duplication. Clients were told that they had to present the voucher to receive a free sample or even to buy drugs. The added advantage of this system was that it insured that clients would become familiar with the distribution location and workers would become familiar with them.

There is general agreement that the TNT crackdown altered considerably street-level dealing in Bushwick. Drug trafficking became less blatant and visible on the streets; as a substantial number of street sellers were arrested and incarcerated. Over the course of the TNT operation, however, street dealers adapted to the intensive enforcement in a variety of ways, including: moving selling locations indoors, shifting selling hours to times when it was believed that TNT might not be operating, using observers to spot TNT officers and vehicles, and by devising schemes to reduce hand-to-hand exchanges.

Although the period of TNT enforcement was associated with a variety of changes in drug market operations, there was a strong perception among the study women, as well as the research team and community residents, that these changes were temporary. Furthermore, our respondents suggest that the overall volume of drug dealing did not decline during the TNT operation, only the locations and intensity (concentration of dealing in a particular location) appeared to have changed. Thus, the deterrence efforts of local law enforcement, too, were short-lived.

HOW DO PEOPLE STOP USING OR SELLING DRUGS?

The natural history of drug use and selling offers some insight into the reasons why criminal punishment may have equivocal deterrent effects. Desistance from drug use (Biernacki, 1986; Waldorf, Reinarman, & Murphy, 1991) and selling (Adler 1985; Padilla, 1992; Williams 1989) is a length and, elaborate social psychological process that involves complex changes in definitions of self and management of one's social interactions. Desistance is a process, with many starts and failures, where relapses are common. For sellers, temporary returns to the material pleasures and excitement of the "life" are not unexpected when the mundane straight life may lead to boredom or financial problems.

Deterrence is not likely to result from a single punishment or any particular event in a sequence of encounters with the law. Together with pressures from the law and other highly valued sources (e.g., family), deterrence seems to be a process that unfolds over time. The low return from legal work may discount the rewards of stopping. Arrest, jailing, the hassle of court appearances, and perhaps a term in prison are part of a familiar cycle for drug offenders that is repeated several times in their careers. The deterrent effect of legal intervention is more likely to derive from maintaining a steady pressure over time that interacts with other social pressures to raise the risks/costs of drug involvement.

If desistance is a social psychological process, what are the potential contributions of criminal punishment in advancing the process? Are the marginal gains in deterring future drug crimes worth the costs of mounting a credible deterrent? The redirection of public resources from other areas that also contribute to desistance/treatment, economic and labor policies, education-implies a marginal cost for deterrence. The funds may be better spent on neutralizing the discount for legal financial gain and reducing the demand side of the equation. The weak deterrent effect of incarceration, compared to probation, suggests that similar marginal deterrent effects might be gained from less expensive alternative sanctions and legal pressures that interact with the social processes of desistance.

BALANCING POLICY

The exclusive focus on specific deterrence in the demand side of drug policy discounts important factors that are part of the natural process of desistance from drug use and selling. This focus also discounts the economic context of decisions to persist or desist from drug involvement. Mounting a specific deterrent effect in the face of widespread drug involvement may be an insurmountable challenge for legal institutions. The relocation of sentencing discretion from judges to the legislature, and in turn to prosecutors through their charging decisions, has achieved a uniformity in sentencing that serves political goals but adds little to the deterrent effect of punishment. Can we reasonably expect to jail all drug offenders? And with what effects on crime rates?

The weak effects of punishment may have counter-deterrent effects that breed disrespect for the laws and institutions that the punishments are designed to uphold. The challenge for policy is to contribute to the processes that motivate drug offenders to stop using and selling. This requires a balanced policy that addresses both punishment for law violation and efforts to revalue the gains from legal behaviors.

The limited choices for punishment present an opportunity for balanced policy. The current reliance on the extremes of incarceration and probation offer little substantive choice for judges and policymakers. Instead of questioning the underlying assumptions of specific deterrence, we respond to the limited effects of punishment with more serious punishment. A range of sanctions makes more sense, as does diversifying the substantive elements of sanctions to include "exits" from drug use or selling. For users, linking punishment with expanded treatment options would provide the types of pressures and alternatives that are implied in the desistance literature. For both users and sellers, so would treatments that increase human capital-job skills and education-that are part of the mix of pressures and escape paths that also characterize desistance. The creation of intermediate punishments would respond to the inadequacies of (de facto unsupervised) probation and provide pressures to stop, while limiting uses of incarceration. Expanding the options for sentencing might restore a more rational allocation of punishments that recognizes the varying thresholds and reactivity of offenders to sanctions.

Finally, the deterrent effects of sanctions may benefit from related policies that emphasize the conditions in which deterrence becomes effective-conditions that both provide and revalue legal opportunities for financial gain, increase the costs of illicit gain, and reduce the opportunities for drug use.

Appendix 1

THE SAMPLE

METHODS AND LOCATION

Our research was based primarily on in depth, life-history interviews with 156 women who sold drugs in two New York City neighborhoods, Bushwick, Brooklyn and Washington Heights, Manhattan. The women were recruited from various social settings including: (1) those in state prison for drug sale convictions; (2) those in jail (Rikers Island) for drug sale convictions; and (3) women actively involved in drug selling.

Women currently involved in dealing were recruited through arrangements with fieldworkers active in ethnographic research in Washington Heights and Bushwick (1992-94). These ongoing studies were designed to collect data on drug sales/distribution, drug use and non-drug criminality. Forty percent (N=63) of the interviews were conducted with active offenders.

The sample contains 62 women (40%) incarcerated in state prisons (Bedford Hills and Bayview) and 31 women (20%) incarcerated in jail (Rikers Island). New York State Department of Correctional Services databases were consulted in order to draw the incarceration samples. Female commitments (to Bedford Hills and Bayview Correctional Facilities) for felony drug sales and Rikers Island Jail for misdemeanor sales, during 1992-93, were eligible for study participation. Only women who sold drugs in the target neighborhoods were eligible for inclusion in this study.

For the women residing in the community, interviews were conducted in a neutral location such as a library or a private office in a university. In order to convey the neutrality and anonymity of the study, we avoided offices of either criminal justice agencies or clinical settings. The women were given a generous travel allowance ($10), regardless of the length or duration of their trip. A stipend of $30 for the interview was paid at the conclusion of the interview, although it was not contingent on completion of the interview. For women who were incarcerated, interviews were conducted in a private office within the correctional facility. These women did not receive a stipend due to institutional rules.

Interviews were open-ended, in-depth and, when possible, audio taped. The open-ended technique created a context in which respondents were able to speak freely and in their own words. Furthermore, it facilitated the pursuit of issues that were raised by the women during the interview but were not recognized beforehand by the researchers. The in-depth interview approach enabled us to pursue information about specific events, as well as provide an opportunity for respondents to reflect on those events. As a result, we were able to gain insight into the women's attitudes, feelings and other subjective orientations to their experiences.

Time reference points were used to assist in the recall of information. The method of sequencing the interview into intervals which are meaningful to the respondent has proven quite successful in collecting retrospective, longitudinal data covering long periods of time. The procedure requires that the interviewer work closely with the respondent to structure the period of interest, using corroborative information and memory aids (e.g. life events and associated dates from official records). In this way, criminal behavior patterns and displacement, shifts in the frequency or severity of criminal involvement (lulls, episodes, relapses after lengthy desistance periods) and contributing situational factors (peer group roles, legal or social sanctions, and life events such as the birth of a child or loss of a job) can be temporally anchored over a multiyear period to establish the natural history of criminal behavior and the factors that have affected its course.

Obtaining an independent means to test the validity of at least some portion of the self-report data is particularly desirable for a study of this nature because the information to be collected could easily be subject to exaggeration or lack of recall. In the present research, estimates of individual offending patterns were confirmed independently through official arrest and conviction records. Official records data were used in the interview in order to help reduce response errors. Interviewers mentioned events found in the official record in order to trigger the recall of events and time periods as well as to curtail respondent misrepresentation of criminal activities.

DESCRIPTION OF THE SAMPLE

Respondents typically were minority women (African American or Latino), 31 years old, high school dropouts with two children, possessing limited work experience (see Table A.1). The youngest was 16 years old and the oldest 48; the median age was 30 years.

Three in four were high school dropouts, typically leaving school by eleventh grade. Although most of the respondents had worked in a legitimate job (83%), the median number of total months employed was only 24, the average was 42.97 months. More than four in five respondents (88%) worked in unskilled and semiskilled working-class occupations (e.g., clerical and factory jobs).

Table A.2 shows self-reported lifetime prevalence of drug use, drug selling, and non-drug crimes. Respondents reported that they were engaged in a wide range of criminal and deviant activities. Nearly all said they were experienced drug users. Seventy-two percent were regular crack users (regular use was defined as using the substance a minimum of four times per week), 49% used cocaine regularly and 40% were at some point in time addicted to heroin. Of the 156 women interviewed, 54% (85) had committed at least one violent crime. Thirty-eight percent reported involvement in robbery, 17% reported involvement in burglary, and 33% had committed assault. Seventy-eight percent of the women were involved in nonviolent crime. Incarceration histories varied widely. The median number of incarcerations was 3 (data not shown). However, 16% (N=25) had never been incarcerated (60% of the sample had never been to prison and 22% had never been in jail). The median and mean total time incarcerated was 19.71 and 10 months, respectively.

Table A.1 Sample Characteristics (N=156)

Age (mean)		30.95
Race (%)		
White		6.4
Black		46.1
Hispanic		46.8
other		.6
Education (years completed)		10.8
School Dropout(%)		75.0
Marital Status at Interview (%)		
married/living together		16.7
never married		53.8
other		29.5
Children		
have children (%)		81.0
number (mean)		2.6
Employment History (%)		
never worked		16.7
sales/cashier/foodworker		20.5
clerical		23.1
health aide		5.8
trade/factory		23.7
Problems while in School	Prevalence (%)	Age at initiation (mean)
fighting	56	10.28
weapons possession	17	13.52
truancy	88	13.73
Family Problems (%)		
someone arrested		60
substance abuse		66
family mental health		30

Table A.2 also shows lifetime participation rates and average initiation age in drug selling by drug type. Most (81%) of the women had sold crack. About half (52% and 45%) had sold heroin and cocaine, respectively. The mean age of initiation into dealing was before 25 years of age. Most had been selling for at least five years.

Table A.2 Crime, Drug Use And Selling History (N=156)

Non-Drug Crimes	Prevalence (%)	Age at initiation
auto theft	19	19.40
shoplifting	58	17.38
forgery	29	23.24
prostitution	44	24.23
assault	33	20.86
robbery	38	22.15
burglary	17	24.52
weapons possession	47	19.64

Drug Used	Prevalence (%)	Age at initiation
alcohol	94	14.37
marijuana	95	15.02
inhalants	18	14.37
hallucinogens	36	17.79
PCP	36	19.04
stimulants	19	18.76
depressants	14	19.14
cocaine	88	20.16
crack	83	24.92
heroin	55	21.86

Drug Sold	Prevalence (%)	Age at initiation	Mean # months
cocaine	45	23.55	64.68
crack	81	25.79	42.24
heroin	52	24.26	69.84
marijuana	27	15.02	30.60
other	12	24.39	61.12

Appendix 2

THE RELATIONSHIP BETWEEN DRUG DEALING AND OTHER MONEY MAKING ACTIVITIES

As we have discussed, the emergence of street markets in cocaine powder and crack presented new income generation options and strategies for women. In the previous heroin markets, income strategies for many women centered on a variety of hustles and petty crimes for others, it was involvement in prostitution (Rosenbaum, 1981; Valentine, 1975; Miller, 1986). Like women heroin users two decades earlier, women involved in cocaine and crack relied on diverse income-producing strategies to support expensive or heavy drug use. For some women, dealing was one element in a repertoire of hustling activities and sources of illegal income. Drug selling was done for money, as part of social activity, and as a way of obtaining a supply of drugs (Hunt, 1990).

Although many women remained disadvantaged in gendered street networks, others, such as Denise and Jocorn, constructed high income careers in illegal work that insulated them from the exploitative and destructive behaviors that characterize heavy cocaine and crack use. Signs of the changing status of women in drug markets were evident in the relatively high incomes some achieved, and the relatively insignificant role of prostitution in generating income (Fagan, 1994; Sommers and Baskin, 1993).

Stephanie's preference for dealing was typical among the women we studied:

> You see, as a prostitute or a hooker, you know, I don't know. For me it's like, uh, you would rather sell drugs or even rob somebody than to perform a service. The last thing I wanted to do is lay down for somebody. I'd rather deal or rip people off.

The opportunities for producing income through drug selling in cocaine markets offered choices that reduced their involvement in hustling, petty crimes and sex markets for income. This suggests that drug dealing was an important intervening factor which modified the relationship between heavy drug use and other criminal activities, including prostitution.

In this appendix, we examine, through **quantitative analysis**, the relationships between drug use and the associated cost-support activities of crime and drug dealing. We provide data across two time periods. The analyses reported below test the parameters of the model shown in Figure I. This model is an adaptation of the addiction career models studied previously by Speckart and Anglin (1986) and Anglin and Speckart (1986). In Figure I, the φ coefficients represent covariances of the exogenous or independent variables, and the y coefficients represent the causal influences exerted by these variables on the endogenous or dependent variables. Exogenous variables are represented by a I and are measures derived from the Time I period, while endogenous variables are represented by a II and are the Time II measures. The ψ coefficients represent residual variances ($\psi 11$, $\psi 12$, $\psi 22$, $\psi 33$, $\psi 44$, $\psi 55$), and residual covariances ($\psi 12$, $\psi 13$, $\psi 14$, $\psi 15$, $\psi 23$, $\psi 24$, $\psi 25$, $\psi 34$, $\psi 35$, $\psi 45$) of the endogenous variables. As noted by Anglin and Speckart (1986):

> ... residual covariances represent the degree of linear relationship between the unexplained portions (residuals) of the dependent variables. A residual covariance is therefore an indication of the amount of covariance between a pair of dependent variables which is not attributable to the influences exerted on them by their mutual predictors in the model (p. 359).

A more detailed explanation of conventions used in causal modeling diagrams is provided by James et al. (1982).

Figure I represents a manifest-variable model, that is, one without latent variables. The present modeling approach therefore does not have the statistical benefits inherent in specifying unmeasured or latent variables from multiple indicators. However, previous research using similar models to the one in Figure I has shown that it produces parameter estimates of causal influences which are similar to those estimated in the context of a latent-variable model (Speckart and Anglin, 1986).

Table A2.1 shows the means and standard deviations. The Time I variables represent the year the respondents initiated their involvement in drug selling and the Time II variables represent three years subsequent to their initiation. The drug selling career data cover the time period of January 1988 - February 1994.

Table A2.1 Means of Variables Used in the Model

Variable	T1	SD	N	T2	SD	N
Drug Expense	1431	1668	140	3206	1427	147
Dealing Income	3346	7228	156	5280	9885	152
Crime Income	970	1366	102	609	566	51
Public Transfer Income	137	75	46	133	78	47
Work Income	332	212	18	311	199	23

Means and standard deviations reflect weekly dollar amounts.

It should be noted that causal inferences based on the present modeling results are not the same as definitive confirmation of direct causal relationships in a rigorous sense. Since the data are nonexperimental in nature, causal associations in the present results may always be ascribed to other factors. For example, the relationship documented between prior dealing and subsequent drug use may be caused by a third variable (e.g., availability) which exerts a direct longitudinal influence over both of these measures. Similar rationales may be formulated as rival explanations for any of the observed significance in parameter estimates.

It is also important to note, that the study data consist of retrospective information. Any inferences drawn here have to be considered conditional on the fact that the subjects were dealing drugs at the time of being recruited into the sample (or immediately prior to their incarceration). Thus, the career progression observed here is circumscribed by that fact. Considering the narrow confines of our empirical data, it is hardly necessary to point out the limits of generalizabilty. Our analysis refers to woman deeply involved in drug selling and immersed in a street subculture. The fact that all the women in this study experienced a lengthy period of drug use and drug selling does not justify the conclusion that this process occurs with all female drug users and sellers. There are undoubtedly other scenarios. Nonetheless, the present results represent a clarification of some dynamic relationships of cost-support activities across time which are relevant to the understanding of behavior at critical phases of drug use and drug selling careers.

Table A2.1 shows that drug expenses, crime and dealing incomes rose significantly across time periods. Incomes from legal work and public transfers remained virtually unchanged. The table also shows that the number of women involved in crime declined as dealing income increased. The shift in the mean levels indicate that major changes are occurring in behavioral propensities of the women at the aggregate level.

However, change in means do not necessarily offer evidence regarding behavioral instability at the individual level, that is, in a correlational sense. For example, assessing the "stability" of drug use and crime behaviors on the basis of means and percentages over successive time intervals may be problematic, since means and percentages may fluctuate dramatically, while predictability in terms of linear relationships across time may be very substantial. Conversely, means and percentages may remain constant on an aggregate group level, while the rank ordering across time among individuals may fail to show a corresponding stability (Anglin and Speckart, 1986). To infer stability correctly, a correlational approach is required which relates individuals' levels of drug use and crime at a given point in time with their subsequent level at a later point in time in the context of an appropriate model (Kessler and Greenberg, 1981).

We used structural equation modeling to test the causal relationships between drug use and the associated income generation activities of drug dealing, crime, legal work, and public transfers. Log transformations were used to adjust for the highly skewed distributions for drug expenses, drug selling and crime incomes. The self-reported data are further complicated by differences in time at risk. Time at risk is defined as the number of days in the community and not in a secure facility. Days-at-risk corrections were applied to drug expenses, drug selling and crime incomes before taking the logarithms. For each time period, self-reported costs and incomes were divided by months at risk. This gave the total drug expenses, drug selling and crime incomes that would have occurred in 365 days at risk. The distribution of the months at risk variable engendered "ceiling" effects; most respondents (68%) were found in the 100% category of this variable. That is, 68% of the respondents had zero days of incarceration during the forty-eight month period for which drug dealing data were reported, and therefore were fully "at risk" for participation in dealing and non-drug crime. Eighty-six percent of the sample were in the community ("at risk") for 80% of the possible "crime days." Thus, it is unlikely that the adjusted data account for the skewed distribution in the drug and non-drug crime variables. The modeling results are provided in Table A2.2.

Statistical significance is determined by the ratio of the parameter estimate to its standard error (.05 level if the ratio exceeds 1.96 and .01 level if it exceeds 2.58).[9] The model is "fully-identified," meaning that, since the number of observed correlations to be accounted for is exactly equal to the number of parameters to be estimate, a perfect fit is obtained. Therefore, no goodness-of-fit indices are appropriate for this model; rather, the results which are relevant are the estimates of the model parameters as indications of causal influence.

The results indicate that the effects of prior drug use on all subsequent variables (except Time 2 drug use) were nonsignificant. In contrast, prior dealing had a facilitating effect on later drug use and significant negative effects on subsequent crime income generation and legal work. Income from crime and legal work during Time 1 had no significant effects on subsequent variables. Public transfer income at Time 1 had a significant negative effect on subsequent crime income.

---

[9] The parameters, in and of themselves, do not indicate strength of association between factors. It is the critical ratio between the parameter estimate and its standard error that reflects statistical significance.

Table A2.2 Model Parameter Estimates

Effects across time periods

Drug-use effects	
Drug Expense T1 - Drug Expense T2	.723 (.052)**
Drug Expense T1 - Dealing Income T2	.007 (.040)
Drug Expense T1 - Crime Income T2	.044 (.097)
Drug Expense T1 - Public Transfers T2	.059 (.045)
Drug Expense T1 - Work Income T2	-.026 (.036)
Dealing effects	
Dealing Income T1 - Drug Expense T2	.064 (.032)*
Dealing Income T1 - Dealing Income T2	.107 (.025)**
Dealing Income T1 - Crime Income T2	-.052 (.026)*
Dealing Income T1 - Public Transfer T2	.003 (.028)
Dealing Income T1 - Work Income T2	-.050 (.022)*
Crime effects	
Crime Income T1 - Drug Expense T2	.067 (.038)
Crime Income T1 - Dealing Income T2	.010 (.029)
Crime Income T1 - Crime Income T2	.498 (.072)**
Crime Income T1 - Public Transfer T2	-.003 (.033)
Crime Income T1 - Work Income T2	.000 (.027)
Public Transfer effects	
Public Transfer T1 - Drug Expense T2	.053 (.049)
Public Transfer T1 - Dealing Income T2	-.084 (.068)
Public Transfer T1 - Crime Income T2	-.225 (.092)*
Public Transfer T1 - Public Transfer T2	.909 (.043)**
Public Transfer T1 - Work Income T2	.028 (.034)
Work effects	
Work Income T1 - Drug Expense T2	-.082 (.060)
Work Income T1 - Dealing Income T2	.043 (.046)
Work Income T1 - Crime Income T2	.099 (.111)
Work Income T1 - Public Transfer T2	-.067 (.052)
Work Income T1 - Work Income T2	.964 (.041)**

Effects within time periods

Simultaneous effects	
Drug Expense T1 - Dealing Income T1	.037 (.058)
Drug Expense T1 - Crime Income T1	.322 (.120)*
Drug Expense T1 - Public Transfer T1	.031 (.088)
Drug Expense T1 - Work T1	-.126 (.107)
Dealing Income T1 - Crime income T1	.134 (.066)*
Dealing Income T1 - Public Transfer T1	-.146 (.140)
Dealing Income T1 - Work T1	-.023 (.122)
Crime Income T1 - Public Transfer T1	.035 (.119)
Crime Income T1 - Work T1	-.018 (.125)
Public Transfer T1 - Work T1	-.115 (.112)

Table A2.2 Model Parameter Estimates

Effects within time periods

Residual Variances	
Drug Expense T2	.898 (.107)**
Dealing Income T2	.547 (.082)**
Crime Income T2	.538 (.200)*
Public Transfer T2	.645 (.093)**
Work Income T2	.312 (.074)**
Residual Covariances	
Drug Expense T2 - Dealing Income T2	.115 (.056)*
Drug Expense T2 - Crime Income T2	.003 (.080)
Drug Expense T2 - Public transfer T2	-.043 (.080)
Drug Expense T2 - Work T2	.079 (.080)
Dealing Income T2 - Crime Income T2	-.098 (.050)*
Dealing Income T2 - Public Transfer T2	-.008 (.080)
Dealing Income T2 - Work T2	.046 (.080)
Crime Income T2 - Public Transfer T2	-.017 (.080)
Crime Income T2 - Work Income T2	-.011 (.060)
Public Transfer T2 - Work Income T2	.034 (.080)

Standard errors are given in parentheses.
* Significant, $p < .05$.
** Significant, $p < .01$.

All the stability coefficients are significant. The stability coefficients indicate the extent to which later behaviors are a linear function of, or can be extrapolated from, earlier measures of these behaviors. It is clear upon inspection of these parameters in conjunction with the means in Table 5 that large changes in means may nonetheless represent a condition of stability in terms of predictability over time. For example, in proceeding from Time 1 to Time 2, drug expenses increase at the aggregate level while maintaining a significant degree of stability, suggesting that drug expenses increase predictably after dealing was initiated as a function of its pre-dealing level.

With regard to the simultaneous effects only drug use and crime and dealing and crime were significant. This indicates that there was a linear relationship between drug use and crime and dealing and crime during the initiation phase of drug selling. Two residual covariances were also significant; indicating that drug use and dealing were directly related and dealing and crime inversely related subsequent to the initiation of drug selling.

Overall, drug dealing appears to have suppressed future non-drug crime activity. This finding suggests that during periods of increased drug use, dealing activities obviated other non-drug crime activities (as well as involvement in legal work). In light of the nonsignificant relationship between crime income at Time 1 and dealing income at Time 2, the findings support the notion that dealing was the preferred source of income support (particularly support of drug costs). The findings also suggest that early in the dealing career, the women were not predisposed toward any particular income generation activity. However, latter on in their careers, they were definitely polarized toward dealing. Specifically, inspection of the significant contemporaneous relationships indicate that in periods of reduced dealing income, crime activities were needed to support drug use behaviors. On the other hand, during periods of increased dealing activity criminal involvement declined even in the face of increasing drug use.

Finally, the significant relationship between prior dealing and future drug use suggests that the strength of addiction was influenced not only by earlier drug use patterns. Immersion in deviant lifestyles, especially affiliation with drug dealing networks, increased opportunities to expand drug use.

The development of a cocaine economy created opportunities for drug selling that did not exist in the smaller, more stable heroin markets. The changing social and economic structures of inner city neighborhoods also created the possibility of changes in the gender roles that in the past constrained women's options for status and income within street drug networks. At one time, women were excluded from selling by rigid gender roles and male hegemony in deviant street networks. The expanding cocaine economy neutralized these social processes that in the past consigned them to secondary roles in street networks. The combination of these factors enabled women either to circumvent gender roles in street drug networks and form new drug selling organizations, or pursue independent careers in drug selling.

Selling also helped women avoid the types of street hustling, including prostitution, that characterized women's income strategies in earlier drug eras. In the past, the worlds of drug use, drug dealing, prostitution, theft, and other hustles comprised the "life" of people within active street networks (French, 1993; Bourgois and Dunlap, 1993). Illegal businesses providing goods and services historically formed the heart of the economy of the "life." While women were consigned secondary, gender-specific roles in these businesses in the past, the size and seemingly frantic activity of the current drug markets helped create new ways for women to participate in street networks. Their involvement in drug selling at high income levels defied the gendered norms and roles of the past, where drug dealing income was an incidental income source often mediated by domestic partnerships. The expansion of drug markets in the cocaine economy provided new ways for women to escape their limited roles, statuses and incomes in previous eras.

In contemporary cocaine markets, drug selling exerted strong influences on income, and their choices of income strategies often shape women's involvement in other crimes. There is evidence of tradeoffs between licit and illicit activities, but investments in licit work were weak at the outset and diminished after onset of cocaine smoking. Entry into cocaine smoking or selling smokable cocaine intensified the illicit endeavors in which they already were active. In the social context of crack use, it is not surprising that street crime continued to be an important part of the "life," and an important income source for women who used crack.[10] Their declining income share from legal work suggests that their attachments to licit labor markets were easily broken as their involvement in cocaine selling intensified.

Low educational levels and short work histories made high incomes from legal work generally unattainable for women sellers. Rather than being drawn

---

[10] Since the relationship between dealing and crime was far from perfect, the findings should not be interpreted to mean that "women drug users who deal don't steal."

from licit work to drug selling, people who chose to sell drugs had few skills that were attractive to putative employers in a service or skilled labor economy. Legal work was a weak option for income, and drug selling seemed to be an appropriate match for this surplus labor pool. Recent data on the declining economic position of even full-time workers further explains women's decisions to pursue illegal incomes that significantly exceeded their expectations from legal work (New York Times, 1994). Drug incomes also were financially more lucrative than other types of crime.

Entry into crack and cocaine sales also were important turning points for their social relations. The trajectories of crime and drug behaviors for women sellers reflected a shift in their social and economic relations. Their *economic* lives placed them increasingly in *social* worlds where they were distanced both from legal work and the health and safety risks of prostitution.[11] Their everyday economic lives centered around drugs. They became immersed in street networks where their social interactions were increasingly limited to people involved in these economic and social behaviors. Their social roles and identities, as well as their primary sources of status and income, were increasingly defined within these street networks. Accordingly, with decreasing social contacts with legal work, these women became immersed in street networks, a process that for many women users led to engulfment in street roles that were defined by their status as drug users (Stephens 1991).

Whatever the income benefits from drug selling, the structural factors related to income and work options may have truncated the natural developmental processes where women might otherwise have made transitions from one stage in the life course to the next. Few women in this study had moved on from careers in drugs to other social roles such as work, school, or marriage. Options for transitions were limited by structural circumstances, especially limited options for licit incomes or improving their prospects in a loose labor market. Their weak job skills created a comparative

---

[11] Women sellers seemed to avoid or reduce their dependence on prostitution (and other street crimes) as an income source, minimizing both their exposure to HIV and to the violence and victimization intrinsic to prostitution (Goldstein et al., 1992). But involvement in drug selling continues to carry with it risks for violence (Fagan and Chin, 1990) and a variety of legal sanctions more serious than the penalties for prostitution (or theft) (Roberts, 1993). Thus, women in the cocaine economy face Hobbesian choices regarding incomes and careers in illegal work. While achieving gender parity in the occupational hazards of drug selling, women drug sellers avoid the disproportionate risks to women from prostitution and drugs-for-sex transactions (Ouellet et al., 1993; Ratner, 1993).

disadvantage in the workplace. The relatively high incomes (for some) from drug selling may have discounted the value of other options in licit work. The low marriage capital of males was a disincentive to entering domestic partnerships. For women users who were active in sex markets, there were few economic or social exits from immersion in those networks.

Viewing women's involvement in drug markets in economic and career terms suggests their agency in decisions charting illicit behaviors over the life course. Earlier deterministic conceptions of women and drugs described a passive decline into street roles of hustling, prostitution, and a secondary social status in worlds dominated by men. In contemporary drug markets, women's participation in drug selling suggests that they made career decisions based, in part, on economic logic and an econometric evaluation of career options, and in part, on social interests. Decisions were made in a world of constrained options. Compared to legal work and options for domestic arrangements, returns from illicit work suggest a fairly rational evaluation of their career options. Although these choices brought risks of victimization and legal hustles, income and social satisfaction seemed to provide a strong motivation.

REFERENCES

Adler, Patricia, (1985) *Wheeling and Dealing: An Ethnography of an Upper-Level Dealing and Smuggling Community.* New York: Columbia University Press.

Adler, Patricia, (1992) The Post Phase of Deviant Careers: Reintegrating Drug Traffickers. *Deviant Behavior* 13:103-26.

Agar, Michael, (1973) *Ripping and Running: A Formal Ethnography of Urban Heroin Addicts.* New York: Seminar Press.

Anderson, Elijah, (1990) *Streetwise.* Chicago: University of Chicago Press.

Anderson, Elijah, (1994) The code of the streets, *The Atlantic Monthly*, May: 81-94.

Anglin, M. Douglas, & Hser, Yih-Hing (1987) Addicted women and crime. *Criminology* 25: 359-97.

Anglin, M. Douglas, & G. Speckart, (1986) Narcotics use, property crime, and dealing. *Journal of Quantitative Criminology* 2:355-375.

Bachman, Jerald, P. O'Malley & J. Johnston, (1978) Adolescence to adulthood-Change and stability in the lives of young men. *Youth in Transition.* vol 6. Ann Arbor, MI: Institute for Social Research.

Baskin, Deborah, Sommers, Ira, & Fagan, Jeffrey, (1993) The political economy of female violent street crime. *Fordham Urban Law Journal* 20: 401-407.

Becker, Howard S., (1963) *Outsiders: Studies in the Sociology of Deviance.* New York: Free Press.

Belenko, Steven A., Fagan, Jeffrey, & Chin, Ko-lin., (1991) Criminal justice responses to crack. *Journal of Research in Crime and Delinquency* 28: 55-74.

Biernacki, Patrick, (1986) *Pathways from Addiction.* Philadelphia: Temple University Press.

Biernacki, Patrick and Waldorf, Dan, (1981) Snowball sampling: Problems and techniques of chain referral sampling. *Sociological Methods and Research* 10: 141-163.

Blackburn, M., D. Bloom and R. Freeman, (1990) The Declining Economic Position of Less Skilled American Men. In Gary Burtless (ed.) *A Future of Lousy Jobs? The Changing Structure of U.S. Wages.* Washington, DC: The Brookings Institution.

Blom, Maria, & van den Berg, T., (1989) A typology of the life and work styles of 'heroin-prostitutes'." In *Growing Up Good: Policing the Behavior of Girls in Europe,* edited by Maureen Cain. London: Sage.

Bluestone, B., M. Stevenson & C. Tilly, (1991) *The deterioration of labor market prospects for young men with limited schooling: assessing the impact of "demand side" factors.* Paper presented at the eastern Economics association Meetings, Pittsburgh.

Bourgois, Phillipe, (1989) In search of Horatio Alger: Culture and ideology in the crack economy. *Contemporary Drug Problems* 16: 619-650.

Bourgois, Phillipe, (1995) In search of respect: Selling crack in El Barrio. New York: Cambridge University Press.

Bourgois, Phillipe, & Dunlap, Eloise, (1993) Excorsing sex-for-crack: An ethnographic perspective from Harlem. In *Crack Pipe as Pimp: An Ethnographic Investigation of Sex-for-Crack Exchanges,* edited by Mitchell S. Ratner. New York: Lexington Books.

Boyle, John, & Brunswick, Ann, (1980) What happened in Harlem? Analysis of a decline in herion use among a generation unit of urban black youth. *Journal of Drug Issues* 10: 109-130.

Brown, Lyn Mikel and Carol Gilligan, (1992) *Meeting at the Crossroads: Women's Psychology and Girls' Development.* New York: Ballantine Books.

Bureau of Justice Statistics, (1992) *Prisoners in 1991* (BJ Bulletin NCJ-134729). Washington, D.C.: U. S. Department of Justice, Bureau of Justice Statistics.

Campbell, Anne, (1984) *The Girls in the Gang.* New York: Blackwell.

Campbell, Anne, (1993) *Men, Women and Aggression.* New York: Basic Books.
Case, A. & L. Katz, (1990) *The company you keep: The effect of family and neighborhood on disadvantaged youths.* Unpublished manuscript. Cambridge: Harvard University, Kennedy School of Government.
Caspi, Avshalom, Donald Lyman, Terrie Moffitt, and Phil Silva, n.d. Unraveling Girls' Delinquency: Biological, Dispositional, and Contextual Contributions to Adolescent Misbehavior, unpublished manuscript.
Chaiken, J., (1988) *Street-level drug enforcement: Examining the issues.* Washington, D. C.: U. S. Department of Justice, National Institute of Justice.
Chavez, Ernest, Ruth Edwards and E.R. Oetting, (1989) Mexican American and White American School Dropouts' Drug Use, Health Status, and Involvement in Violence, *Public Health Reports* 104:594-604.
Chiricos, Ted, (1987) Rates of Crime and Unemployment: An Analysis of Aggregate Research. *Social Problems* 334:187-212.
Chesney-Lind, Meda, (1986) Women and crime: The female offender. *Signs* 12: 78-96.
Cohen, Bernard, (1980) *Deviant Street Networks: Prostitutes in New York.* Lexington, MA: Lexington Books.
Colten, Mary Ellen, & Marsh, Judith E., (1984) A sex roles perspective on drug and alcohol use by women. In *Sex Roles and Psychopathology*, edited by Cathy Spatz Widom. New York: Plenum Press.
Corcoran, Mary, & Parrott, Susan, (1992) Black women's economic progress. Paper presented at the Research Conference on the Urban Underclass: Perspectives from the Social Sciences. Ann Arbor, Michigan: June.
de la Rosa, Mario, (1990) Introduction: Exploring the Substance Abuse-Violence Connection," in de la Rosa et al. (eds.) *Drugs and Violence: Causes, Correlates and Consequences.* Rockville, MD: National Institute on Drug Abuse.
de la Rosa, Mario, Elizabeth Lambert and Bernard Gropper, (1990) *Drugs and Violence; Causes, Correlates, and Consequences.* Rockville, MD: National Institute on Drug Abuse.
Dembo, Richard, Linda Williams, Werner Wothke, James Schmeidler, Alan Getreu, Estrelita Berry, Eric Wish and Candice Christensen, (1990) The Relationship between Cocaine Use, Drug Sales, and Other Delinquency among a Cohort of High-Risk Youths Over Time," in de la Rosa, et al.,

(eds.) *Drugs and Violence: Causes, Correlates and Consequences.* Rockville, MD: National Institute on Drug Abuse.

Division of Criminal Justice Services, (1988) *New York State: Trends in felony drug offense processing, 1983-87.* Albany: Author.

Division of Criminal Justice Services, (1990) *New York State: Trends in felony drug offense processing, 1985-89.* Albany: Author.

Douthat, S., (1988) Holiday Season Brings the Blues to Incarcerated Mothers. *The Brunswick News*, p. 2.

Duany, J., (1994) *Quisqueya on the Hudson: The Transnational Identity of Dominicans in Washington Heights.* City College of New York, CUNY Dominican Studies Institute.

Dunlap, Eloise, (1992) The impact of drugs on family life and kin networks in the inner-city African-American single parent household. Pp. 99-145 in *Drugs, Crime and Social Isolation: Barriers to Urban Opportunity*, edited by Adele Harrell and George Peterson. Washington DC: The Urban Institute Press.

Dunlap, Eloise, Johnson, Bruce D., Sanabria, Harry, Holliday, Elbert, Lipsey, Vicki, Barnett, Maurice, Hopkins, William, Sobel, Ira, Randolph, Doris, and Chin, Ko-lin, (1990) Studying crack users and their criminal careers: The scientific and artistic aspects of locating hard-to-reach subjects and interviewing them about sensitive subjects. *Contemporary Drug Problems* 17: 121-144.

Elder, Glenn H., Jr., (1985) Perspectives on the Life Course. Pp. 23-49 in *Life Course Dynamics*, edited by G.H. Elder, Jr. Ithaca, NY: Cornell University Press.

Eldred, C.A., & Washington, M.N., (1976) Interpersonal relationships in heroin use by men and women and their role in treatment outcome. *International Journal of the Addictions* 11:117-130.

Elliott, D. and H. Voss, (1974) *Delinquency and Dropout.* Lexington, MA: Lexington.

Epstein, E., (1977) *Agency of fear.* New York: Putnam.

Erickson, Patricia, & Murray, Glenn, (1989) Sex differences in cocaine use and experiences: A double standard revived? *American Journal of Drug and Alcohol Abuse* 15:135-152.

Ettorre, Elizabeth, (1992) *Women and substance use.* New Brunswick, NJ: Rutgers University Press.

Fagan, Jeffrey, (1992) Drug selling and licit income in distressed neighborhoods: The economic lives of drug users and drug sellers." In *Drugs, Crime and Social Isolation: Barriers to Urban Opportunity*, edited by Adele Harrell and George Peterson. Washington DC: The Urban Institute Press.

Fagan, Jeffrey, (1994) Legal and illegal work: Crime, work and unemployment. Paper presented at *Metropolitan Assembly on Urban Problems: Linking Research to Action* Northwestern University, Center for Urban Affairs and Policy Research.

Fagan, Jeffrey, (1996) Legal and illegal work: Crime, work and unemployment. In Burton Weisbrod and James Worthy (eds.) *Dealing with Urban Crisis:Linking Research to Action*. Evanston, IL: Northwestern University Press.

Fagan, Jeffrey, and Chin, Ko-lin, (1990) Violence as regulation and social control in the distribution of crack. In *Drugs and Violence*, edited by Mario de la Rosa, Elizabeth Lambert, and Bernard Gropper. National Institute on Drug Abuse Research Monograph No. 103. DHHS Pub. No. (ADM)90-1721. Rockville, MD: U.S. Department of Health and Human Services.

Fagan, Jeffrey, and Chin, Ko-lin, (1991) Social processes of initiation into crack use and dealing. *Journal of Drug Issues* 21 (2): 313-343.

Fagan, Jeffrey and Richard Freeman, (1994) Crime and Work. Unpublished. Newark, NJ: Rutgers University, School of Criminal Justice.

Fagan, J., E. Piper & M. Moore, (1986) "Violent Delinquents and Urban Youth," *Criminology* 24:439-472.

Fagan, J. and S. Wexler, (1987) Crime in the Home and Crime in the Streets: The Relation Between Family Violence and Stranger Crime. *Violence and Victims* 2:5-21.

Farley, Reynolds, (1987) Disproportionate Black and Hispanic unemployment in U.S. metropolitan areas. *American Journal of Economics and Sociology*. 46:129-50

Farley, Reynolds, (1988) After the starting line: Blacks and women in an uphill race. *Demography* 25:447-495.

Farley, Reynolds, & Allen, Walter R., (1987) *The Color Line and the Quality of Life in America*. New York: Russell Sage Foundation.

Faupel, Charles, (1991) *Shooting Dope: Career Patterns of Hard-Core Heroin Users*. Gainsville: University of Florida press.

Faupel, Charles & Karl Klockeers, (1987) Drugs-crime connections: Elaborations from life histories of hardcore heeroin addicts. *Social Problems* 4:54-68.

Feldman, H., M. Agar & G. Beschner, (1979) *Angel dust: An ethnographic study of PCP users.* Lexington, MA: Lexington Books.

Felson, M., (1986) Linking Criminal Choices, Routine Activities, Informal Social Control, and Criminal Outcomes, in Cornish, D. and R. Clarke (eds.) *The Reasoning Criminal.* New York: Springer-Verlag, 119-128.

Felson, M. and L. Cohen, (1980) Human Ecology and Crime: A Routine Activity Approach, *Human Ecology* 8:389-406.

File, K.N., (1976) Sex roles and street roles. *International Journal of the Addictions* 11:263-268.

Freeman, Richard, (1992) Crime and the Employment of Disadvantaged Youths. In George Peterson and Wayne Vroman (eds.) *Urban Labor Markets and Job Opportunities.* Washington, DC: Urban Institute Press.

Freeman, Richard, (1983) Crime and Unemployment. In James Q. Wilson (ed.), *Crime and Public Policy.* San Francisco: Institute for Contemporary Studies Press.

French, John, (1993) Pipe dreams: Crack and the life in Philadelphia and Newark. In *Crack Pipe as Pimp: An Ethnographic Investigation of Sex-for-Crack Exchanges,* edited by Mitchell S. Ratner. New York: Lexington Books.

Glick, R. and V. Neto, (1977) *National Study of Women's Correctional Programs.* Washington, D.C.: Government Printing Office.

Goerdt, J. & J. Martin, (1989) The impact of drug cases on case processing in urban trial courts. *State Court Journal* 4-12.

Goldstein, Paul J., (1979) *Prostitution and Drugs.* Lexington, MA: Lexington

Goldstein, Paul J., (1985) The drugs-violence nexus: a tri-partite conceptual framework. *Journal of Drug Issues* 15: 493-506.

Goldstein, Paul J., (1989) Drugs and violent crime. Pp. __ in *Pathways to Criminal Violence,* edited by Neil Weiner and Marvin Wolfgang. Beverly Hills: Sage Publications.

Goldstein, Paul J., Lipton, Douglas, Preble, Edward, Sobel, Ira, Miller, Thomas, Abbott, W., Paige, W., & Soto, F., (1984) The marketing of street heroin in New York City. *Journal of Drug Issues* 14: 553-66.

Goldstein, Paul J., Spunt, Barry, Belluci, Patricia, & Miller, Thomas, (1991) Volume of cocaine use and violence: A comparison between men and women. *Journal of Drug Issues* 21: 345-67.

Goldstein, Paul J., Ouellet, Laurence J., & Fendrich, Michael, (1992) From bag brides to skeezers: An historical perspective on sex-for-drugs behavior. *Journal of Psychoactive Drugs* 24:349-61.

Golub, Andrew, & Johnson, Bruce D., (1993) Cohort differences in drug use pathways to crack among current crack users in New York City. Unpublished. New York: National Development and Research Institutes

Gusfield, J., (1975) The futility of knowledge: The relation of social science to public policy toward drugs. *Annals of the American Academy of Political and Social Science* 417:1-28.

Hagan, John, (1989) *Structural Criminology*. New Brunswick, NJ: Rutgers University Press.

Hagan, John, (1993) The Social Embeddedness of Crime and Unemployment. *Criminology* 31:465-492.

Hagan, John, (1994) *Crime and disrepute*. Thousand Oaks, CA: Pine Forge Press.

Hagan, John and Alberto Pallioni, (1990) The Social Reproduction of a Criminal Class in Working Class London, circa 1950-1980. *American Journal of Sociology* 96:265-299.

Hagan, John, J. Simpson & A. Gillis, (1987) Class in the household: A power-control theory of gender and delinquency. *American Journal of Sociology* 92:788-816.

Hagedorn, John & P. Macon, (1988) People and Folks: Gangs, Crime and the Underclass in a Rustbelt City. Chicago: Lake View Press.

Hamid, Ansley, (1990) The political economy of crack-related violence. *Contemporary Drug Problems* 17 (1): 31-78.

Hamid, Ansley, (1992) Drugs and patterns of opportunity in the inner city: The case of middle-aged, middle-income cocaine smokers. In *Drugs, Crime and Social Isolation: Barriers to Urban Opportunity*, edited by Adele Harrell and George Peterson. Washington DC: The Urban Institute Press.

Hser, Yih-Hing., Anglin, M.Douglas, & McGlothlin, William H., (1987) Sex differences in addict careers. 1. Initiation of use. *American Journal of Drug and Alcohol Abuse* 13: 33-57

Hughes, G., (1983) The concept of crime. In S. Kalish (ed.) *Encyclopedia of Crime and Justice*.
Hunt, Dana, (1990) Drugs and consensual crimes: Drug dealing and prostitution. In *Drugs and Crime*, edited by Michael Tonry and James Q. Wilson. Chicago: University of Chicago Press.
Inciardi, James A., (1979) Heroin use and street crime. *Crime and Delinquency* 25: 335-346.
Inciardi, James A., Lockwood, Dorothy, & Pottieger, Anne E., (1993) *Women and Crack Cocaine*. New York: MacMillan.
James, L., R. Mulaik & J. Brett, (1982) *Causal Analysis: Assumptions, Models, and Data*. Beverley Hills, CA: Sage.
Jarjoura, G. Roger, (1993) Does Dropping out of School Enhance Delinquent Involvement? Results from a Large Scale National Probability Sample, *Criminology* 31:149-172.
Jargowsky, Paul A., and Bane, Mary Jo, (1990) Ghetto poverty: Basic questions. In *Inner City Poverty in the United States*, edited by Lawrence Lynn and Michael G.H. McGeary. Washington DC: National Academy Press.
Jargowsky, Paul A., and Bane, Mary Jo, (1991) Ghetto poverty in the United States: 1970-80. In *The Urban Underclass*, edited by Christopher Jencks and Paul E. Peterson. Washington DC: The Brookings Institution.
Jencks, Christopher, (1991) Is the American underclass growing? In *The Urban Underclass*, edited by Christopher Jencks and Paul E. Peterson. Washington DC: The Brookings Institution.
Jensen, G. and D.Brownfield, (1986) Gender Lifestyles and Victimization: Beyond Routine Activity Theory," *Violence and Victims* 1:85-89.
Jessor, R. and S. Jessor, (1977) *Problem behavior and psychosocial development: A longitudinal study of youth*. New York: Academic Press.
Johnson, Bruce D., Goldstein, Paul J., Preble, Edward, Schmeidler, James Lipton, Douglas, Spunt, Barry, & Miller, Thomas, (1985) *Taking Care of Business: The Economics of Crime by Heroin Abusers*. Lexington, MA: Lexington Books.
Johnson, Bruce D., Williams, Terry, Dei, Kojo, & Sanabria, Harry, (1990) Drug abuse and the inner city: Impacts of hard drug use and sales on low income communities. In *Drugs and Crime*, edited by James Q. Wilson and Michael Tonry. Chicago: University of Chicago Press.

Johnson, Bruce D., Hamid, Ansley, & Morales, Edmundo, (1990) Emerging models of crack distribution. In *Drugs and Crime: A Reader,* edited by Thomas Mieczkowski. Boston: Allyn-Bacon.

Kaplan, J., (1983) *The hardest drug: Heroin and public policy.* Chicago: University of Chicago Press.

Kasarda, John D., (1988) Jobs, migration and emerging urban mismatches. In *Urban Change and Poverty,* edited by Michael G.H. McGeary and Lawrence E. Lynn. Washington DC: National Academy Press.

Kasarda, John D., (1989) Urban industrial transition and the underclass. *The Annals of the American Academy of Political and Social Science* 501:26-47.

Kessler, Ronald & D. Greenberg, (1981) *Linear panel analysis: Models of quantitative change.* New York: Academic press.

Kirschenman, J. & K. Neckerman, (1991) "We'd Love to Hire Them, But...: The Meaning of race for Employers," In *The Urban Underclass.* edited by C. Jencks and P. Peterson. Washington, DC: The Brookings Institution.

Kleiman, Mark A.R., (1992) *Against Excess: Drug Policy for Results.* New York: Basic Books.

Kozel, Nicholas J., & Adams, Edgar H. (eds.), (1985) *Cocaine Use in America: Epidemiological and Clinical Perspectives.* National Institute on Drug Abuse Research Monograph No. 61. DHHS Pub. No. (ADM)85-1414. Rockville, MD: U.S. Public Health Service.

LaGrange, Randy and Helene Raskin White, (1985) Age Differences in Delinquency: A Test of Theory, *Criminology* 23:19-45.

Laub, John and R. Sampson, (1993) Turning points in the life course: Why change matters to the study of crime. *Criminology* 31:301-326.

Lauderback, David, Hansen, Joy, & Waldorf, Dan, (1992) "Sisters are doin' it for themselves": A Black female gang in San Francisco. *The Gang Journal* 1:57-92.

Lauritsen, Janet L. Robert J. Sampson and John Laub, (1991) The Link between Offending and Victimization among Adolescents," *Criminology* 20:265-291.

Lewis, Carla, B. Johnson, A. Golub, & E. Dunlap, (1992) Studying crack abusers: Strategies for recruiting the right tail of an ill-defined population. *Journal of Psychoactive Drugs 24:323-336.*

Liebow, Elliot, (1967) Tally's corner: A study of negro streetcorner men. Boston, MA: Little, Brown and Company.

Loeber, Rolf and P. Wikstrom, (1993)) Individual pathways to crime in different types of neighborhoods. In D. Farrington (ed.) *Integrating individual and ecological aspects of crime.* Stockholm, Sweden: The national Council for Crime Prevention.

Longshore, Douglas, Anglin, M. Douglas, Hsieh, Shih-Chao, and Annon, Kiku, (1993) Sexual behaviors and cocaine preference among injection heroin users in Los Angeles. *Journal of Drug Issues* 23:363-374.

MacCoun, Robert, and Reuter, Peter, (1992) Are the wages of sin $30 an hour? Economic aspects of street-level drug dealing. *Crime and Delinquency* 38: 477-91.

Maher, Lisa, & Curtis, Richard, (1993) Women on the edge of crime: Crack cocaine and the changing contexts of street level sex work in New York City. *Crime, Law and Social Change* 18: 221-258.

Mare, Robert D., & Winship, Christopher, (1991) Socioeconomic change and the decline of marriage for blacks and whites. In *The Urban Underclass*, edited by Christopeher Jecks and Pault E. Peterson. Washington DC: The Brookings Institution.

Massey, Douglas, & M. Eggers, (1990) The ecology of inequality: Minorities and the concentration of poverty, 1970-80. *American Journal of Sociology* 95:1153-1188.

Mieczkowski, Thomas, (1986) Geeking up and throwing down: Heroin street life in Detroit. *Criminology* 24: 645-666.

Miller, Eleanor, (1986) *Street Woman.* Philadelphia: Temple University Press.

Moore, Joan, (1992a) *Going Down to the Barrio: Homeboys and Homegirls in Change.* Philadelphia: Temple University Press.

Moore, Joan, (1992b) Institutionalized Youth Gangs: Why White Fence and El Hoyo Maravilla Change so Slowly. In J. Fagan (ed.) *The Ecology of Crime and Drug Use in Inner Cities.* New York: Social Science Research Council.

Moore, M., (1977) *Buy and bust.* Lexington, MA: Lexington Books.

Moss, S., (1986) Women in Prison: A Case of Pervasive Neglect. *Women and Therapy* 5:5.

Moss, P. & C. Tilly, (1991) *Why black men are doing worse in the labor marker: A review of supply-side and demand-side explanations.* Paper prepared for the Social Science Research Council, Committee on Research on the Urban Underclass, Subcommittee on Joblessness and the Underclass. New York: Social Science research Council.

Murphy, Sheila, Waldorf, Dan & Reinarman, Craig, (1991) Drifting into Dealing: Becoming a cocaine seller. *Qualitative Sociology* 13: 321-343.
Musto, D., (1990) *An American Disease: Origins of Narcotics Control.* New York: Oxford University Press.
Myers, M., (1989) Symbolic policy and the sentencing of drug offenders. *Law and Society Review 23:295-315.*
New Jersey Supreme Court, (1990) *Proceeding of the 1990 New Jersey State Judicial Conference.* Trenton: Administrative Office of the Courts.
New York City Police Department, (1990) *Statistical report: Complaints and arrests, 1989.* New York: Office of Management Analysis and Planning.
New York Times, (1989a) Report from the field on an endless war. March 12, Section IV, p. 5.
New York Times, (1989b) Selling milk, bread, and cocaine in New York. March 30, B1.
New York Times, (1994) Women doing crime, women doing time. July 3, E3.
Office of National Drug Control Policy, (1989) National Drug Control Strategy. Washington, DC: Office of National Drug Control Policy, The White House.
Oliver, Melvin, (1995) Commentary. In M. Belinda Tucker and C. Michell-Kernan (eds.) *The decline in marriage among African Americans.* New York: Russell Sage Foundation.
Ouellet, Lawrence J., Wiebel, W. Wayne, Jimenez, A.D., & Johnson, W.A., (1993) Crack cocaine and the transformation of prostitution in three Chicago neighborhoods. In *Crack Pipe as Pimp: An Ethnographic Investigation of Sex-for-Crack Exchanges,* edited by Mitchell S. Ratner. New York: Lexington Books.
Padilla, Felix, (1992) *The Gang as an American Enterprise.* Boston, MA: Northeastern University Press.
Pipher, Mary, (1994) Reviving Ophelia: Saving the selves of adolescent girls. New York: Ballantine Books.
Pettiway, Leon, (1987) Participation in crime partnerships by female drug users: The effects of domestic arrangements, drug use, and criminal involvement. *Criminology* 25:741-766.
Preble, Edward, & Casey, John J., Jr., (1969) Taking care of business: The heroin user's life on the street. *International Journal of the Addictions* 4:1-24.

Ratner, Mitchell, (1993) Sex, drugs, and public policy: Studying and understanding the sex-for-crack phenomenon. In *Crack pipe as pimp: An ethnographic investigation of sex-for-crack exchanges*, edited by Mitchell Ratner. New York: Lexington Books.

Reinerman, C. & H. Levine, (1989) Crack in context: Politics and media in America's latest drug scare. *Contemporary Drug Problems* 16:535-578.

Reinarman, Craig, Waldorf, Dan, & Murphy, Sheila, (1989) The call of the pipe: Freebasing and crack use as norm-bound episodic compulsion. Paper presented at the Annual Meeting of the American Society of Criminology, Reno, Nevada, November.

Reuter, Peter, MacCoun, Robert, & Murphy, Patrick, (1990) Money from Crime. Report R-3894. Santa Monica, CA: The Rand Corporation.

Ricketts, Errol, & Sawhill, Isabel, (1988) Defining and measuring the underclass. *Journal of Policy Analysis and Management* 7:316-325.

Roberts, Dorothy E., (1991) Punishing drug addicts who have babies: Women of color, equality, and right of privacy. *Harvard Law Review* 194: 1419-82.

Roman, L., (1990) Jailed Mothers Risk Losing Their Kids. *New Directions for Women*. March/April:12.

Rosenbaum, Marsha, (1981) *Women and Heroin*. New Brunswick, NJ: Rutgers University Press.

Rowe, David and Bill Gulley, (1992) Sibling Effects on Substance Use and Delinquency, *Criminology* 30:217-223.

Sampson, Robert J., (1992) Family management and child development: Insights from social disorganization theory. In *Facts, Forecasts, and Frameworks*, edited by Joan McCord, 63-92. New Brunswick, NJ: Transaction Publishers.

Sampson, Robert J., (1986) Effects of socioeconomic context on official reaction to juvenile delinquency. *American Sociological Review* 51:876-85.

Sampson, R. & W. B. Groves, (1989) "Community Structure and Crime: Testing Social-Disorganization Theory," *American Journal of Sociology* 94:774-802.

Sampson, Robert J., and Laub, John H., (1990) Crime and deviance in the life course. *Annual Review of Sociology* 18: 63-84.

Sampson, Robert J., and Laub, John H., (1993) *Crime in the Making*. Cambridge: Harvard University Press.

Sassen-Koob, Sassia, (1989) New York City's informal economy. In *The Informal Economy: Studies in Advanced and Less Developed Countries*, edited by Alejandro Portes, Manuel Castells, and Lauren A. Benton. Baltimore: Johns Hopkins University Press.

Sassen-Koob, Sassia, (1991) The informal economy. In *Dual city: Restructuring New York*, edited by John Mollenkop & Manuel Castells. New York: Russell sage.

Schur, E., (1971) *Labeling Deviant Behavior: Its Sociological Implications*. New York: Harper & Row.

Schuster, Charles, (1990) Forward, in De La Rosa, Mario, E. Lambert and B. Gropper (eds.) *Drugs and Violence: Causes, Correlates and Consequences*. Rockville, MD: National Institute on Drug Abuse.

Shannon, L., (1986) Ecological Effects of the hardening of the inner city. In Metropolitan Crime Patterns, edited by Robert Figlio, Simon Hakim and George Rengert. Monsey, NY: Willow Tree Press.

Sherman, L., (1990) Police crackdowns. In N. Morris and M. Tonry (eds.) *Crime and Justice: An annual review of research*. (vol 12) Chicago: University of Chicago Press.

Shover, Neil, (1985) *Aging Criminals*. Newbury Park, CA: Sage.

Siegel, Ronald K., (1987) Cocaine smoking: Nature and extent of coca paste and cocaine freebase abuse. In *Cocaine: A Clinician's Handbook*, edited by Arnold .M. Washton and Mark Gold, New York: The Guilford Press.

Silver, G., (1979) *The dope chronicles: 1850-1950*. San Francisco: Harper and Row.

Skogan, Wesley, (1990) *Disorder and Decline: Crime and the Spiral of Decay in American Neighborhoods*. New York: Free Press.

Sommers, I. and D. Baskin, (1992) Sex, Race, Age and Violent Offending. *Violence and Victims* 7:191-202.

Sommers, I. and D. Baskin, (1993) The Situational Context of Violent Female Offending. *Journal of Research in Crime and Delinquency* 30:136-162.

Sowder, B. and M. R. Burt, (1980) *Children of Heroin Addicts: An Assessment of Health, Learning, Behavioral, and Adjustment Problems*. New York: Praeger.

Sparks, Richard F., Greer, Alexandra, and Manning, Sally, (n.d.) Theoretical Studies, Volume 2: Crime as Work. Final Report, Grant 80-IJ-CX-0060, National Institute of Justice. Washington DC: U.S. Department of Justice.

Speckart, George & D. M. Anglin, (1986) Narcotics use and crime: A causal modeling approach. *Journal of Quantitative Criminology* 2:3-38.

Spitz, Harry I., & Rosecan, Jeffrey S., (1987) Cocaine reconceptualized: Historical overview." In *Cocaine Abuse: New Directions in Treatment and Research,* edited by Henry I. Spitz and Jeffrey S. Rosecan. New York: Brunner-Mazel.

Stattin, H. and D. Magnusson, (1990) *Pubertal Maturation in Female Development* Hillsdale, N.J.: Erlbaum.

Steffensmeier, Darrell, (1983) Organization properties and sex-segregation in the underworld: Building a sociological theory of sex differences in crime. *Social Forces* 61: 1010-1032.

Stephens, Richard C., (1991) *The Street Addict Role: A Theory of Heroin Addiction.* Albany, NY: State University of New York Press.

Sterk, Claire, E. and Kirk W. Elifsen, (1990) Drug-Related Violence and Prostitution, in De La Rosa, et al (eds.) *Drugs and Violence: Causes, Correlates and Consequences.* Rockville, MD: National Institute on Drug Abuse.

Straus, Murray, R. Gelles & S. Steinmetz, (1980) *Behind closed doors: Violence in the American family.* New York: Doubleday.

Sullivan, Mercer, (1989) *Getting Paid.* Ithaca, NY: Cornell University Press.

Sutherland, Edward, with Chic Conwell, (1937) *The Professional Thief.* Chicago: University of Chicago Press.

Taylor, D., R. Taub & B. Peterson, (1986) Crime, community organization, and causes of neighborhood decline. In Metropolitan Crime Patterns, edited by Robert Figlio, Simon Hakim and George Rengert. Monsey, NY: Willow Tree Press.

Thornberry, T., M. Moore and R.L. Christenson, (1985) The Effect of Dropping Out of High School On Subsequent Criminal Behavior. *Criminology* 23:3-18.

Tienda, Marta, (1989) Neighborhood effects and the formation of the underclass. Paper presented at the Annual Meeting of the American Sociological Association, San Francisco, August.

Trebach, A., (1982) *Sanctions and social deviance: The question of deterrence.* New York: Praeger.

Valentine, Bettylou, (1978) *Hustling and Other Hard Work: Life Styles in the Ghetto.* New York: Free Press.

Vicusi, W. Kip, (1986) The Risks and Rewards of Criminal Activity: A Comprehensive Test of Criminal Deterrence. *Journal of Labor Economics* 4:317-340.

Wacquant, Loic D., & Wilson, William J., (1989) The costs of racial and class exclusion in the inner city. *The Annals of the American Academy of Political and Social Science* 501:8-25.

Waldorf, Dan, (1973) *Careers in Dope.* Englewood Cliffs, NJ: Prentice Hall.

Waldorf, Dan, Reinarman, Craig, & Murphy, Sheila, (1991) *Cocaine Changes: The Experiences of Using and Quitting.* Philadelphia: Temple University Press.

Waterston, Alisse, (1993) *Street Addicts in the Political Economy.* Philadelphia: Temple University Press.

Watters, John K, and Biernacki, Patrick., (1989) Targeted sampling: Options for the study of hidden populations. *Social Problems* 6: 416-30.

Williams, Terry., (1989) *Cocaine Kids.* Reading, MA: Addison-Wesley.

Williams, Terry., (1992) *Crackhouse.* Reading, MA: Addison-Wesley.

Wilson, William J., (1987) *The Truly Disadvantaged.* Chicago: University of Chicago Press.

Wilson, William J., (1991) Studying inner-city social dislocations: The challenge Of public agenda research. *American Sociological Review* 56: 1-14.

Wilson, William J., (1996) *When work disappears: The world of the new urban poor.* New York: Alfred Knopf.

Wilson, William J. and Allan Abrahamse, (1992) Does Crime Pay? *Justice Quarterly* 9:359-377.

Wolfgang, M. E., (1958) *Patterns in criminal homicide.* Montclair, NJ:

Zahn, M., (1989) Homicide in the Twentieth Century: Trends, Types and Causes, In: T. Gurr (ed.) *Violence in America, Volume I: The History of Crime.* Newbury Park, CA: Sage, 1989.

Zimmer, L., (1987) Operation Pressure Point. An Occasional Paper of the Center for Crime and Justice, New York University School of Law. New York: New York University School of Law.

Zimring, F. & G. Hawkins, (1992) *The search for rational drug control.* Berkeley: Cambridge University Press.

INDEX

A

addiction, 2, 3, 6, 18, 38, 50, 55, 77, 78, 85, 88, 89, 96, 98, 103, 105, 106, 111, 118, 129, 152, 158
adolescence, 44, 49, 50, 51, 52, 53, 56, 80, 86, 128
aggression, 37, 46
alcohol problems, 38

B

battered woman, 122
Bedford-Stuyvesant, 34
Blacks, 28, 38, 136, 167
boyfriends, 2, 16, 18, 65
Brooklyn, 8, 28, 31, 32, 33, 47, 50, 80, 135, 136, 137, 138, 145
brothers, 2, 39, 40, 52, 53, 91
burglary, 10, 90, 98, 111, 112, 147, 149
Bushwick, 8, 9, 28, 30, 31, 32, 33, 34, 35, 36, 38, 56, 107, 135, 136, 137, 138, 139, 140, 145

C

child abuse, 6, 37
childhood, 34, 37, 44, 50, 80
childhood experiences, 44
class transformation, 26
cocaine, 3, 4, 5, 9, 10, 16, 18, 19, 20, 21, 23, 27, 33, 39, 40, 53, 54, 60, 61, 62, 63, 64, 76, 78, 79, 81, 82, 90, 95, 111, 122, 127, 128, 129, 130, 135, 137, 147, 148, 149, 151, 152, 158, 159, 160, 166, 169, 172, 173, 175
community networks, 6
conventional lifestyles, 110, 116, 119
crack, 1, 5, 6, 9, 10, 18, 19, 20, 21, 23, 25, 31, 33, 39, 41, 43, 54, 57, 59, 60, 61, 64, 66, 69, 78, 81, 82, 84, 85, 86, 90, 92, 93, 94, 95, 96, 97, 98, 100, 101, 102, 103, 104, 106, 112, 117, 128, 129, 130, 131, 137, 138, 140, 147, 148, 149, 151, 159, 160, 164, 166, 167, 169, 171, 174
crack arrests, 25
crime, 5, 8, 17, 18, 22, 24, 25, 26, 27, 31, 34, 38, 50, 51, 66, 67, 69, 70, 73, 74, 75, 76, 77, 79, 80, 81, 86, 89, 90, 102, 104, 106, 109, 111, 112, 113, 115, 116, 117, 118, 119, 120, 121, 122, 124, 125, 129, 135, 142, 147, 152, 154, 155, 158, 159, 160, 163, 165, 168, 170, 171, 172, 173, 176
criminal punishment, 132, 133, 141
criminal sanctions, 129, 132, 133, 134
criminalization, 50

D

delinquency, 38, 44, 169, 174
demographic changes, 6, 28
demoralization, 35
depression, 19, 20, 107
desistance, 8, 11, 109, 110, 114, 116, 117, 118, 119, 120, 121, 122, 123, 124, 125, 141, 142, 146
deterrence, 121, 129, 135, 140, 141, 142, 176
deviant lifestyles, 128, 158
deviant social networks, 18
dignity, 36
disinvestment, 31, 34
distressed communities, 7, 26, 27, 34, 127
distressed neighborhoods, 26, 167
domestic relationships, 18
Dominicans, 31, 135, 136, 138, 166
drinking, 8, 35, 45, 47, 54, 55, 56, 76, 117
drug abuse, 2, 6, 7, 35, 41, 57, 92, 101, 106, 132
drug arrestees, 131
drug crimes, 131, 132, 135, 141
drug distribution, 4, 5, 7, 16, 32, 33, 34, 41, 66, 67, 70, 76, 79, 99, 101, 133, 136
drug economy, 4, 23, 24, 25, 31, 133, 135
drug epidemics, 131
drug experimentation, 45, 51
drug markets, 1, 2, 3, 6, 7, 8, 15, 16, 19, 20, 21, 27, 33, 55, 56, 60, 63, 64, 71, 82, 83, 85, 86, 104, 134, 136, 137, 151, 159, 161
drug offenders, 130, 131, 132, 133, 134, 141, 142, 173
drug policy, 132, 134, 142
drug sales, 9, 25, 40, 52, 59, 145
drug selling, 2, 3, 4, 5, 6, 7, 8, 9, 12, 16, 20, 21, 22, 24, 27, 51, 58, 59, 65, 70, 71, 82, 104, 113, 127, 128, 129, 133, 135, 139, 145, 147, 148, 152, 153, 154, 158, 159, 160, 161
drug supermarket, 33, 136, 137
drug trafficking, 73, 129, 130, 138
drug transactions, 34, 69

drug use, 3, 4, 7, 9, 10, 11, 12, 16, 17, 18, 19, 20, 21, 22, 25, 33, 41, 43, 51, 55, 56, 59, 60, 67, 70, 81, 84, 104, 106, 119, 128, 129, 130, 132, 133, 134, 137, 141, 142, 143, 145, 147, 151, 152, 153, 154, 155, 158, 159, 160, 167, 169, 170, 173
drugs, 1, 2, 3, 4, 5, 7, 8, 10, 11, 12, 16, 17, 18, 19, 20, 21, 24, 25, 31, 33, 34, 35, 41, 42, 47, 49, 51, 54, 55, 56, 57, 58, 60, 61, 62, 63, 65, 66, 67, 68, 69, 70, 76, 77, 78, 79, 80, 82, 83, 85, 89, 90, 92, 93, 94, 95, 96, 98, 100, 101, 102, 103, 104, 105, 106, 109, 110, 111, 112, 113, 117, 119, 120, 130, 131, 132, 133, 134, 135, 136, 138, 140, 145, 151, 152, 153, 160, 161, 166, 169, 174

E

economic decay, 6
economic destabilization, 22
economic marginalization, 23, 26
edginess, 20
education, 6, 28, 66, 75, 120
emotional stability, 36
employment, 4, 6, 21, 23, 24, 42, 73, 75, 76, 77, 79, 80, 81, 102, 127
employment opportunities, 73

F

family members, 37, 46, 52, 58, 65, 84, 91, 93, 96, 124
family networks, 6, 38
family obligations, 7
family relations, 38, 43
friendships, 59

G

gender roles, 3, 82, 127, 158
ghettoization, 31

H

health care, 36, 75
heroin, 2, 3, 8, 10, 15, 16, 17, 18, 19, 20, 21, 23, 25, 27, 31, 33, 38, 40, 41, 52, 59, 60, 61, 64, 66, 80, 82, 84, 95, 96, 100, 127, 129, 131, 136, 138, 147, 148, 149, 151, 158, 166, 168, 172, 173
Hispanic, 28, 30, 31, 32, 38, 111, 113, 148, 167
HIV, 9, 18, 20, 88, 160
homicide, 24, 25, 177
husbands, 2, 16, 18
hustling, 17, 18, 56, 77, 79, 83, 84, 151, 152, 159, 161

I

identity, 8, 76, 85, 109, 110, 116, 117, 118, 119, 120, 122, 123, 124, 125
immigrants, 28, 29, 63
incarceration, 25, 114, 115, 129, 130, 133, 134, 135, 141, 142, 145, 153, 155
initiation into, 7, 8, 10, 11, 24, 45, 51, 54, 55, 127, 128, 148, 167
inner cities, 3, 4, 18, 19, 21, 22, 23, 27, 73
inner city, 4, 6, 15, 24, 25, 26, 37, 43, 49, 74, 82, 127, 128, 158, 169, 170, 175, 177
inner city families, 37
institutionalization, 51
intense drugs, 20

J

job opportunities, 73

L

labor market access, 4, 24
Latinos, 31, 136
loneliness, 38, 42

M

Manhattan, 8, 28, 29, 60, 69, 80, 138, 145
marijuana, 4, 18, 20, 33, 40, 46, 53, 55, 60, 66, 90, 129, 149, 150
mental health problems, 40, 41, 87
motivation, 12, 23, 122, 161

N

n.d., 44, 49, 165, 175
needles, 20, 21
neighborhood disintegration, 22
neighborhoods, 4, 8, 9, 19, 21, 22, 23, 24, 27, 28, 29, 31, 33, 34, 35, 36, 38, 80, 82, 104, 127, 128, 135, 136, 138, 145, 158, 172, 173
New York City, 2, 5, 8, 15, 19, 21, 22, 23, 24, 25, 28, 29, 30, 31, 50, 127, 131, 134, 137, 145, 168, 169, 172, 173, 175
noncriminal identities, 119
Non-Hispanic Black, 30
Non-Hispanic White, 30

O

opiates, 25, 131

P

parental supervision, 7, 55
peer relations, 6, 15
personal history, 6
personal safety, 35
pimps, 2, 17, 92
political power, 32
poor neighborhoods, 4, 23, 24, 25, 128
poverty, 4, 6, 22, 23, 24, 26, 29, 30, 32, 127, 128, 170, 172
prison populations, 131
prosocial activities, 38, 56, 96
prostitutes, 2, 3, 35, 164
Puerto Ricans, 135, 136

punishment, 25, 121, 123, 124, 129, 130, 134, 135, 137, 141, 142

Q

queen pins, 2, 63

R

racial inequality, 26
racial segregation, 22, 23
renegotiation, 124
residential mobility, 22
role engulfment, 8, 85
role models, 6, 24, 127
rundown housing, 34

S

school experiences, 44, 45, 48
search for excitement, 7
secondary deviance, 2
secondary labor market,, 80
self-esteem, 36, 46, 106
sex markets, 3, 152, 161
sexuality, 49
shoplifting, 17, 51, 55, 60, 83, 98, 129, 149
single parenthood, 50, 51
social identity, 116, 123, 124
social institutions, 36, 49
social isolation, 26, 96
social labeling, 49
social networks, 12, 17, 18, 25, 26, 34, 58, 59, 60, 61, 65, 110, 122, 123
social processes, 6, 8, 11, 12, 59, 82, 104, 127, 141, 159
social regulation, 23
socialization, 6, 24, 38, 45, 127

street crime, 2, 6, 7, 37, 44, 46, 51, 95, 96, 98, 101, 111, 159, 160, 163, 170
street deviance, 8, 51, 55
street drug networks, 20, 82, 127, 159
street life, 16, 48, 55, 56, 88, 89, 95, 105, 106, 108, 110, 111, 113, 116, 119, 172
street networks, 5, 7, 8, 21, 25, 27, 65, 74, 82, 85, 109, 127, 151, 159, 160
substance abuse, 6, 38, 40, 128, 129, 148

T

treatment program, 117, 118, 119

U

underclass communities, 6
unemployment, 24, 29, 32, 41, 73, 167
urban drug markets, 2

V

values, 27, 36, 85
victimization, 6, 7, 17, 50, 71, 96, 103, 160, 161
violence, 7, 8, 26, 31, 34, 35, 40, 46, 50, 58, 63, 66, 67, 68, 69, 70, 71, 79, 86, 96, 97, 101, 103, 113, 128, 129, 137, 160, 169

W

Washington Heights, 8, 9, 28, 29, 30, 31, 35, 36, 63, 145, 166
welfare benefits, 23

DATE DUE			
GAYLORD			PRINTED IN U.S.A.

Lewis & Clark College - Watzek Library
3 5209 00688 9766